W9-ADF-897

PENGUIN PLAYS

THE BASIC TRAINING OF PAVLO HUMMEL *and* STICKS AND BONES

David Rabe was born in 1940 in Dubuque, Iowa. He lived and went to school in Dubuque until 1962, when he graduated from Loras College and went east to begin graduate work toward an M.A. in theater at Villanova University. Drafted into the army in 1965, he served until 1967. In 1968 he started work on a sequence of plays and took a job as a feature writer for the *New Haven Register Sunday Pictorial Magazine*, where he won an Associated Press award for feature writing. In the fall of 1971 he returned to Villanova, functioning this time as a teacher in the Graduate Theatre Department. In the spring of 1971 Joseph Papp gave Rabe his first professional production at the New York Shakespeare Festival Public Theater. The play was *The Basic Training of Pavlo Hummel*, which won an Obie Award for Distinguished Playwriting (and was successfully revived on Broadway in 1977, starring Al Pacino). Since then the New York Shakespeare Festival has given productions of *Sticks and Bones* (which won a Tony for Best Play on Broadway in 1972 and was also done on television), *The Orphan, In the Boom Boom Room*, and *Streamers*. In 1974 *The Basic Training of Pavlo Hummel* and *Sticks and Bones* were honored by the American Academy of Arts and Letters. Mr. Rabe won the New York Drama Critics Award in 1976 for *Streamers*, the Best American Play, as well as the Drama Desk Award for Outstanding New Play. Rabe's plays have also won a *Variety* Award, the Elizabeth Hull–Kate Warriner Drama Guild Award, and the John Gassner Outer Critics Circle Award.

Gramley Library
Salem College
Winston-Salem, NC 27108

WITHDRAWN

The Basic Training of Pavlo Hummel

AND

Sticks and Bones

Two Plays by DAVID RABE

PENGUIN BOOKS

Gramley Library
Salem College
Winston-Salem, NC 27108

Penguin Books Ltd, Harmondsworth,
Middlesex, England
Penguin Books, 625 Madison Avenue,
New York, New York 10022, U.S.A.
Penguin Books Australia Ltd, Ringwood,
Victoria, Australia
Penguin Books Canada Limited, 2801 John Street,
Markham, Ontario, Canada L3R 1B4
Penguin Books (N.Z.) Ltd, 182–190 Wairau Road,
Auckland 10, New Zealand

First published in the United States of America by
The Viking Press 1973
First published in Canada by
The Macmillan Company of Canada Limited 1973
Viking Compass Edition published 1973
Reprinted 1973, 1974 (twice), 1976,
1977 (twice)
Published in Penguin Books 1978
Reprinted 1980

Copyright © David Rabe, 1969, 1972, 1973
All rights reserved

LIBRARY OF CONGRESS CATALOGING IN PUBLICATION DATA
Rabe, David.
    The basic training of Pavlo Hummel and Sticks and
bones.
    (Penguin plays)
    I. Rabe, David. Sticks and bones. 1978. II. Title.
[PS3568.A23B3 1978]   812'.5'4   78-17308
ISBN 0 14 048.137 0

Printed in the United States of America by
The Murray Printing Company, Westford, Massachusetts
Set in Electra

Acknowledgment is made to Charles E. Tuttle Co., Inc.,
for a selection from Vietnamese Legends
by George F. Schultz

Photographs by Friedman-Abeles

Except in the United States of America,
this book is sold subject to the condition
that it shall not, by way of trade or otherwise,
be lent, re-sold, hired out, or otherwise circulated
without the publisher's prior consent in any form of
binding or cover other than that in which it is
published and without a similar condition
including this condition being imposed
on the subsequent purchaser

Alas! This life is like a flower that forms, then fades.
My wife is dead, so I bury her; if I were dead, she would remarry.
If I had been the first to depart, what a great burst of laughter
   would have poured forth.
In my fields a new laborer would work; on my horse a strange rider
   would appear.
My wife would belong to another; my children would have to bear
   anger and insults.
When I think of her, my heart tightens; but I look at her without
   weeping.
The world accuses me of insensibility and remorselessness;
I scoff at the world for nourishing vain griefs.
If I could restore the course of things by weeping,
My tears would flow for a thousand autumns without ceasing.

                             —Vietnamese legend

Life a funny thing.
           —Sonny Liston

Contents

Introduction

Most notions that occur to me as being possibly interpretive of these plays are met in my mind with disapproval. I don't know—or perhaps don't want to know—anything definitive about them. I learned things through their creation, and to a large degree that is what makes them precious to me. I proceeded through a number of years, working on a number of projects, moving from one to the other, doing a first draft of one, a third draft of another, forcing something of each of those days into the work. Whether you write one play or twenty, each contains various histories from various levels of your life. At a certain point in time, I knew nothing of the experiences that would lead me to *Pavlo* or *Sticks and Bones*. At another, later point, they were in me, though essentially unknown—a mix of memory, thought, fantasy. Step number one was dredging them up, getting them onto paper. Secondly came the long haul of the hunt for a stage and for a producer. It seems to me now that a few moments excerpted from each of these ventures might be the best way to bring a reader nearer to my plays, to their genesis and to my feelings about them.

• •

With the first draft of *Pavlo Hummel* completed in the fall of 1968, and the first draft of *Sticks and Bones* begun, I loaned the only existing copy of *Pavlo Hummel* to a director-teacher friend. When I called upon him some time later to retrieve the script, he could not find it. I have blotted out my feelings, yet I know I be-

lieved it would be found. Six or eight weeks afterwards, it was uncovered among old exams and term papers in the office of another
teacher, who claimed he had never seen it.

• •

There were nights in 1967 and 1968 when, after an evening or
date in downtown Philadelphia, I would go to the door of a friend
who lived in the residential area just south of Rittenhouse Square
—a concrete and grass block in Center City Philadelphia—and ring
him awake, for if I had stayed late enough in the go-go bars, or with
my girl, or simply on the street, walking, there was no transportation back to Elliot Street and the room I rented in Bryn Mawr.

So my friend would buzz his downstairs door open and I would
labor up the several flights of stairs, lugging my bag of beer past
huge hallway mirrors that showed me a 2:00 or 3:00 a.m. version of
myself. His door would be open. In the room—the apartment was
an efficiency with one window and a phony fireplace—I would find
pillows and a sheet piled on the floor in the corner, where there
were also a lamp and a table. More often than not, I would light
the lamp to its lowest wattage, look over and smile into the bleary
face of the girl about whom my friend was curled, and settle down
to think a little, hoping I might end up jotting something down. I
might drink a glass of beer, but never more than one until I reached
that point in my scribbling when the urge to stop equaled the sense
of need to get something stated, the need to force some inner fog
of feeling into thought. Often in those nights, I amazed myself.
Not at the quality or art of what I wrote but at the kinds of
thoughts I was having when the feelings that most filled me then,
twined and (I now think) primal, were given a shape in language
that made them ideas I understood instead of shifting phantoms
possessing me.

• •

One night in 1968, on my way to the Showboat Bar in downtown
Philadelphia to hear trumpet-player Hugh Masekela, I was intro-
duced to a black man (whom I never saw or spoke to beyond that
introduction) named Ardell.

• •

The writing I did in college was dominated by an urge to interpret the world to itself, to give the world a sermon that would bring it back to its truest self, for I thought then (and I did indeed believe it) that the history and exact nature of both mankind and the world were known, universal, and eternal.

I no longer write from that urge (though I'm sure some of it lingers) but try to start instead from the wish to discover. Or perhaps from the wish to formulate my discoveries. Or perhaps, even more correctly, from the need to see if I have *made* any discoveries.

● ●

In the spring of 1969 I was accepted by an agent, Jim Bohan. To be acknowledged, finally, by someone working in the professional theater seemed a major event.

● ●

In the summer of 1970, as I was coming to the end of my stint as a feature writer for the *New Haven Register Sunday Magazine,* I packed up my manuscripts, my wife, and what I hoped was a sufficient supply of audacity. Heading north, I traveled up the highway out of Connecticut to Williamstown, Massachusetts, intending to manage a meeting with a young director named Jeff Bleckner, who had never heard of me nor of anything I had written. From various sources, however, I had heard of the quality of his work, and for months the conviction had grown in me that the first step toward production was not sending the manuscripts off in the mail but getting to know directors who were believed in by producers. Because I was acquainted with several people who were Bleckner's friends and working at Williamstown, I thought I had a good chance. He was there rehearsing *Rosencrantz and Guildenstern Are Dead,* which would open after the current *Streetcar Named Desire,* which I was covering for the New Haven paper.

Yet as soon as I arrived, I realized nothing occurring in this weekend would change my situation. Two or three times I saw him from a distance. His rehearsals were closed and the people I knew were busy beyond any interest in me.

On the afternoon of the day we left, my wife and I were sitting in our car in the parking lot behind the theater. In the shade along the rim of a small valley there, Jeff Bleckner, Sam Waterston, and Charlie Siebert were rehearsing. We could not hear them. I could find no words with which to make a reasonable walk up to them. The cliché of inadequate, desperate writer that I felt he would see in my approach held me pressed in my seat.

• •

Not that I went on and on without my own good luck, however. Very early a copy of *Pavlo Hummel* which I sent to the Public Theater mysteriously never returned. A little later I sent *Sticks and Bones*, which was rejected by a director there who liked it, but not enough. I sent him *Pavlo Hummel* and got it back. All this was in 1969. Then in the summer of '70, *Pavlo* got into the hands of Mel Shapiro, who cared about it enough to begin to look for a theater. "Go to the Public Theater," I suggested. That missing copy of *Pavlo* was on Joe Papp's desk. It lay there among the scripts Joe considered possible but oddly difficult. It had lain there for some time. Mel Shapiro's interest now nudged Joe through his doubts, convincing him to give the script a try. The wait began. Mel was directing *The House of Blue Leaves*. By now we were in November '71. The actors' strike hit, delaying *Blue Leaves*. *Pavlo*, then scheduled for February, was pushed back. By the time *Blue Leaves* finally opened in February, Mel had been offered a job directing a new Ionesco play down at the Arena Stage in Washington, D.C. Mel said I should do what I thought best for the play. Joe didn't like to take a director off a play, since a director had to have feeling for the work. Nevertheless, he said, there was a young director named Jeff Bleckner whose work Joe respected. If Jeff liked the play and I felt Jeff understood the play in a way that would let us work together, we would proceed.

• •

When I returned from Vietnam, I was home for some six months before I thought seriously of writing (finally there was nothing else to do with the things I was thinking). But oddly enough, it was a novel rather than a play that I wanted to work on. I had written both plays and novels earlier in my life and my writing came from something in me not dedicated to any one form.

And upon return, theater seemed lightweight, all fluff and meta-phor, spangle, posture, and glitter crammed into a form as rigid as any machine geared to reproduce the shape of itself endlessly. In the way that all machines are unnatural in a natural universe, theatrical form seemed artificial beyond what was necessary.

But then I chanced upon a grant of money, a Rockefeller grant in playwrighting, enough to live on for a year and a half. I remember thinking, "I'll dash off some plays real quick, then focus in on the novel."

But when I sat down to write, regardless of the form, I found it impossible to avoid the things most crowding my mind, and because these memories and ideas were of such extreme value to me, I could deal with them with nothing less than my best effort.

What I am trying to say is simply that if things had turned out differently, I don't know if I would have written what I have in the way I have, but the grant was a playwrighting grant.

• •

Five weeks into rehearsal of *The Basic Training of Pavlo Hummel*, the director, Jeff Bleckner, and I knew there were problems, and knew also the areas in which they lurked. The play spun out of kilter when it hit them, plopped down, and rolled about. Most of the problems were in the second act, but the key to all of them was in a kind of stylistic chasm between the two acts. The basic-training metaphor, meaning "essential" training (and intended to include more in this case than the training given by the army) had not been carried through in the writing or staging. The first act seemed rooted to an inextricable degree in documentary realism, while the second was fragmentary and impressionistic in a way that seemed to make any comprehensive and convincing sense of realism impossible.

So we got Joe Papp in to see a run-through of the show a day or two before he had planned to join us. He was a stranger to me at the time, a man with power enough to put on or not put on my work, or any work. He had closed a show in the Newman theater (one of the stages within the Public Theater complex) to make room for *Pavlo* and I had wondered immediately what the name of the show would be for which he would bring *Pavlo* down.

At the end of the first act, he was pleased though clearly not thrilled. However, less than two minutes into Act Two, he was on his feet and drifting back row by row until he was talking intently with Jeff. An hour and a half later, when the actors had been dismissed, Jeff and I headed, in a state of some apprehension, up the stairs to Joe's office for a sip of scotch and the labor of analysis and judgment. Listing the areas he thought troublesome, Joe batted a thousand, zeroing in precisely on the points we were worried about ourselves. He amazed me with his ability to go to the heart of my play. At this point in our relations, I half expected him to be unable to keep my own play separate from all the others he was reading and working on, yet he had deciphered many of *Pavlo*'s secrets, and the forces that were its substructure.

However, I knew something of the history of *Subject to Fits*, a bizarre, surreal play on which Joe had exerted influence and from which had come a large critical success. Though I had liked *Fits* tremendously when I saw it, I felt *Pavlo* was another breed of beast. I began to fear that Joe was attempting to exert similar influences on *Pavlo*'s more realistic structure, for in the hour that we talked, he urged a breakdown of the linear nature of the play. Theatrically, I understood his position, but felt threatened by any wrenching of *Pavlo*'s essential nature.

When Joe left, he said the next day's rehearsal procedures were entirely up to us, but he had left us with no doubt as to the kinds of changes he wanted. Jeff and I talked late into the night and in the morning found, sadly, that we were ready to do no more than continue talking. Joe called us to a second conference. His question was simple: what scenes in the second act could be moved into the first?

I knew instantly the set-piece sequences that could be lifted and knew also the kind of surreal play that would result. Sensing the pressure of Joe Papp's position and power, I felt a real anger beginning. Not because I had some fixed theory of realistic theater that I wanted to protect, but rather because *Sticks and Bones* with its nonreal style was already written and *The Orphan*, a third play, which moved even further into fantasy and "theatricality," had been drafted. As a result, my need was extreme for *Pavlo* to put down roots in the real. It would be the base from which I moved outward with other work. I felt *Pavlo*, the first written, had to be a play that was primarily about people. Therefore I wanted it done in the theatrical form in which dramatic characters had the best chance of appearing as simply people. With more open anger than I meant to show, I accused Joe of wanting to risk harm to the play in order to avoid appearing in some way outside the current theatrical fashion. Did a realistic play seem to him like an old narrow tie? Did he think form was something you started from or could change on whim like a shirt or tie? The anger hit him, I know, for the air was thick enough with tension to conduct any spark. Jeff later told me that he had thought I was going to throw the typewriter that was there on the desk before me.

Joe calmly explained that little he did was motivated by fashion. All he wanted from us was an effort toward solving our problems more forceful than sitting in a room verbally hashing and rehashing options that were, in reality, physical possibilities. If we moved a scene from one act to another, no law would hold it there if it didn't fit. But our minds were closed with uncertainty, he said, at a time when we could least afford it.

So we changed the position of two second-act scenes, rewriting them only slightly. Another pair of scenes in the second act were fragmented and restaged in a manner that allowed their implications to flow more freely back and forth: the man with one arm and everything amputated below the waist was on stage while Pavlo visited the whorehouse. To draw the metaphor of basic training as ritual throughout the entire fabric of the play, we decided to repeat a first-act drill scene in the middle of the second act and to put a formation at the very start of the second act. Jeff and I worked quietly and, oddly, with confidence. One of the two scenes tried in the first act was moved back to its original position in the second. The actors were patient and hopeful. Joe observed off and on but said little during this process. Once, as I sat leaning forward, wary and watchful for some distortion of the play to occur in the changes we were making, I sensed someone sitting down behind me and spun as if I might be ambushed. Joe was there. "It's a friend," he said. He had snapped us out of our inertia, and once we were off and running, he let us go.

On opening night he came up to me with a letter in which he

stated that, regardless of the critical response to *Pavlo Hummel*, he was grandly pleased. My future work could be done in his theater as long as he had one and I was willing.

•   •

Late one afternoon just after the opening of *Sticks and Bones*, I looked up at the banners bearing the titles of my two plays waving above the Public Theater, and they were colorful and glossed with sunlight.

A block or so later on my walk toward the subway, a bum in a battered blue coat tied at the waist with rope asked me for some change to buy him some wine. And when, because of my expansive mood and my sense of extreme good fortune, I gave him more than even he (with his excellent eye for a soft touch) had dreamed I might, a look of joy came into his eyes that was so pure it made me laugh, and he yelled aloud toward a distant corner where I now saw another bum standing before a man dressed in an overcoat, suit, and tie. "I got it, Henry," my bum was yelling. "I got it. I got it, Henry."

Then he turned to me. "You my friend," he said. And he hugged me. "You my friend." And he was all loose and joyful emotion, his huge old arms around me as I stood there confused and pleased and, in a show of some affection, awkwardly patting on his back. "You my friend," he said again, and we weren't, of course, for he was going to his gutter and I to my plays, but we had had that moment.

•   •

While in Vietnam, I felt I should keep some sort of journal, for I had written things before the service, and hoped to write again. But all my efforts brought me nothing, or very little, and the reasons were many, of course, but essentially two.

I remember once sitting more or less paralyzed over the phrase "artillery rounds" scribbled on a yellow-lined page. Cannon were booming a few miles across the nearby road and dust shook loose in puffs from the tentfolds. My phrase sat on the page like a husk. I was aware acutely, and in a way that makes writing impossible, of the existence of language as mere symbol. In no way could I effect the cannon, the shuddering tent flaps. In an utterly visceral way, I detested any lesser endeavor. The events around me, huge and continual, were the things obsessing me. So I sat staring at the words on the page and the page was yellow on a cot standing on a wooden floor.

In addition, writing requires a kind of double focus that I could not then quite handle. If you encounter an auto accident and then go home to write of it seriously, you must bring your full sensibility to bear upon all elements of that accident. To do this in Vietnam (though there are men who have done it) was a task I didn't try. Not only to see the dead and crippled, the bodies, beggars, lepers, but to replay in your skull their desperation and the implications of their pain (even while they continued on the streets outside), seemed a lunatic journey. I did not go upon it. I was living then in a high, brittle part of my mind. I skimmed over things and hoped they would skim over me. Being brittle, this mental barrier might have broken, for the stipulations of its requisition had been only speedy construction and hardness, yet it held, and proved strong enough to send the sights I saw and all their reverberations bouncing off like moths trying to get to the light beyond the screen.

All I knew in Vietnam were facts, nothing more: all simple facts of such complexity that the job of communicating any part of them accurately seemed impossibly beyond my reach. So I kept no journal and even my letters grew progressively more prosaic, fraudulent, dull, and fewer and fewer. Clichés were welcomed, as they always are when there is no real wish to see what they hide.

•   •

The first person I showed *Pavlo Hummel* to, a director I respected, told me I was wasting my time and should give it up. In anger, I went to work on *Sticks and Bones*.

•   •

We drove to read Clive Barnes' review of *Sticks and Bones* at 2:00 a.m. on opening night, the same night that a *New York Times* truck driver was shot to death on 43rd Street. On his way to the newsstand Jeff walked past the body covered with a blanket. He did not know of the shooting. He returned to tell us someone had been hit by a car.

• •

Casting is always an ordeal because you know that any mistakes you make cannot easily be canceled out. Your wish then is to be clairvoyant, to find in a short glimpse the whole of what an actor can do. Casting is depressing and difficult and there is no way to be really fair to an actor.

I saw Bill Atherton doing John Guare's *House of Blue Leaves* several weeks before we started casting and thought of him immediately for *Pavlo*. We got him to read and at first try he was excellent. He had a Huck Finn mix of innocence, toughness, and mischievousness. We felt he was right, yet we failed to trust our instincts, and went on and on reading other actors for five more weeks.

Joe Fields appeared one day on the recommendation of Ron O'Neal, who was set at the time to do Ardell. The minute Joe walked into the room, I knew he should be in the play. His reading had an authenticity. At the time, however, I was not thinking of him as Sergeant Tower, for whom he had read, so we asked him to read an additional passage, one he had not prepared. He read quickly and poorly and left. Jeff was ready to chalk him off, but I wanted to call him back. A few days later he read again for Sergeant Tower and Jeff also began to detect the quality I had seen. Joe Papp, whom we had called in to affirm our choices, thought Bill Atherton and Ron O'Neal excellent but was unsure of Joe Fields. Without changing his own opinion, however, Papp accepted our choice because of the force of our commitment to it. So the cast was set, it seemed.

Then a week into rehearsal Ron O'Neal got a movie offer and we lost him. He was there one day and gone the next. Panic struck, for our announced opening date was not far away. More importantly, we were already so late in the season, that delay would be more like demise.

Albert Hall was playing a minor part at this point, and it was Jeff's thought to move him up to Ardell. I was uncertain. Al had never acted professionally before and it seemed rash to give him as important a role as Ardell, though his work on the small part was excellent and his commitment was total.

Jeff and I were feeling more than a little desperation: we were caught in the idea that failure would be ruinous. So we sat in the casting office and talked for hours that night, weaving a web of intangibles, hoping to find a hook substantial enough to hold Al Hall in the role of Ardell. But finally nothing was concrete and consistent except Jeff's gut faith in Al's ability. In the end, I trusted that.

A few weeks later all doubts were removed: "Joe Fields," wrote Clive Barnes, "as the amiably honey-voiced tyrant, is very impressive, as is Albert Hall as the elusive Ardell, both mocking and humane. . . . William Atherton had a distinct personal success. Rawboned and awkward, good natured but stupid, Hummel goes through the play like a stifled cry of pain, going to his death like a slaughtered lamb."

•   •

Because I noted in the program that *Sticks and Bones* was done at Villanova as early as 1969, a number of people have concluded that it was written before *Pavlo Hummel*, which received no production whatsoever until Joe Papp did it in 1971. It would seem the assumption beneath this conclusion is that a play is written from start to finish, like a man running a race, that it is then produced, and that the next play is written from start to finish and, of course, produced before anything new is begun. It is a nice, orderly, after-the-fact way of viewing things, and I can see the need for this kind of historical thinking if you're on the receiving end of plays and obliged to state your feelings about their relative merit one to the other; but I doubt seriously if many plays are written that way.

In actuality *Pavlo* was under way long before *Sticks and Bones*. With a full draft of *Pavlo* completed, I began *Sticks and Bones*. With several drafts of *Sticks and Bones* completed, I did a one-acter called *Nor the Bones of Birds*. After another draft of *Pavlo* I dredged up eighty pages of a novel. Then another half-hour one-acter came along. I went back to *Sticks and Bones*, and then on to what I was positive would be the final version of *Pavlo*. About this time the two one-act plays began to seem as if they might fill out into full-lengths. Produced at Villanova, *Sticks and Bones* clearly needed more work. I did a draft based on what I'd learned in production. I did a short story. And along the way, lost (I think) the energies of a story about a girl and her father, and a little play about Admiral Yamamoto being blown out of the air over the Pacific.

•   •

One of the major conflicts between the characters in *Sticks and Bones* is a disagreement about the nature of the world in which they are living, or, in other words, about the kind of language that is used to define experience. David says of the girl he loved, "She was a girl to weigh no more than dust." Ozzie says, "You pronged a yellow fucking whore." The simple, real event is hidden by each character in the language he uses. A play is a world. The language of a play displays and defines the nature of that world. One of the major conflicts of *Sticks and Bones* is whether the world is ordinary, stereotypical, or poetic. As David is poetic, he tries to draw the others toward the poetry in themselves; but as there is madness in poetry, they are reluctant to go.

•   •

The decision to move *Sticks and Bones* to Broadway started in Joe Papp's mind while he was in England and I was in Iowa in late December 1971. Shortly after his return to the States, I talked to him long distance and found out the notion existed as possibility. I had mixed feelings, to say the least, for I was still amazed at the success the play was having at the Public Theater. Returning east, I found that Joe had already begun his search for the right uptown theater. Some bitterness moved in me at this discovery. I feared the life of the play would be seriously endangered and did not understand Joe's reasons for wanting to take the risk. My idea was that perhaps the future of serious theater in New York depended on abandoning Broadway. Let Broadway become the circus it seemed to want to be. Get all playwrights, even the most prestigious, to think of Off Broadway as the place for their work. We were being deluded by our outdated legend about the glamour of Broadway. Good writer after good writer, it seemed, had been foundering on the rocks uptown. Perhaps Broadway was no longer the place where good writing was tested against the best work of others, both current and time-honored.

I told Joe all this and more one morning when he was in a mood he has in which his mind revs more rapidly than anything you're saying. Realizing this made me talk all the faster, yet as I was stating my position, he was unfolding his own. The move would be a planned, protected venture with a goodly sum of money to cushion possible losses and guarantee a run. Our reviews had been all good, so we wouldn't be opening blind. Also, he said, if one regularly observed the three hundred people attending the show downtown, it became quickly clear that they were not a strictly "downtown" or "young" audience. More often than not, they looked like what was termed an "uptown" audience. In addition, the ideas of the play were ideas he wanted the uptown audience exposed to in as large a number as possible.

I agreed, one way or another, with most of what he said. And then there was the appeal of something he hadn't mentioned. The move uptown would put us into a proscenium theater instead of the three-quarter stage we were on at the Anspacher (another of the Public Theater's stages), and during rehearsals it had become clear to me that the play would be at its best in a proscenium. There was nearly reason enough in this for me to accept the move. I went away undecided, thinking. Yet that evening, while talking to a friend who asked how I felt about the move, I answered, "I think it's like trying to make a whore come." Sometime that night I must have decided, however, that I had nerve enough to try it, for when I called Joe it was to agree to go along with his plans. But he was in a mood I could not have anticipated. "It's off," he said. "Until you decide you want it. I woke up at four in the morning last night thinking about what you said. It's a risk I want to take, but it's your play I'm risking even if I protect it as much as I can. So you've got to decide to go or not to go. If we did it and it didn't go, I don't want you coming up to me yelling, 'You sonofabitch, you killed my play.'"

So I had to start all over, but it didn't take so long the second time. Suspended above the two alternatives, I saw I was capable of touching each with one or the other toe. I looked to the one that was a challenge, and then I rocked and swung toward it with the hope in me that the feeling I was taking for courage was not in fact hubris.

Work on the play was a pleasure, for in the proscenium we had more focus and control. The new set was wonderful, giving the sense of space that the play needed. With the audience further away, the actors were freed from the need to "behave" which the intimacy of the Anspacher had forced upon them. Because the play lives in a middle ground between what is thought of in theater terms as "realism" and "fantasy," precise stylization is a crucial production factor, and now this ingredient was more possible. Though it is set in a living room, the play is primarily taking place in theatrical space.

Aesthetically, everything that happened was positive. There were moments, in fact, in which it seemed Jeff was reading my mind about the way I thought a scene should be rearranged in terms of the new space. The actors, who had quite naturally thought that moving to a bigger theater would necessitate a larger playing energy and size found that the reverse was true. Increased focus put subtlety and precision at a premium.

However, no matter what confidence I felt in the new work we were doing, nothing could shake my sense that even if we did our best and won fresh recognition from the critics, we could still sink quickly out of sight. Something more than our good work was needed, though I did not know what it was. I believed, finally, that something beyond my control, something in the area of economics, or advertising, in the psyche of that mysterious phenomenon of the "uptown" audience, or in the powers of Joe Papp would ultimately determine the fate of the play. We had left a neighborhood where the names of plays were in paint or on a banner and bums wandered the street or sat chatting on the curb. Now we were up where pimps and queens paraded, where the names of plays were in flashing lights and you scrambled for business against *Butterflies Are Free* and naked girls (called "nude models") who promised "Exotic Massages" behind the colorful walls of their street-front parlors.

When the first advertisement announcing the move appeared, I felt a hundred insidious and fatal errors had been made within that half-page rectangle of text and design. I sat that Sunday morning parked in front of the drugstore in which I had bought the paper, cursing aloud in rage.

•   •

Julius Novick, who considered *Sticks and Bones* a ". . . failure of some considerable stature . . . ," wondered at one point in his review in the *Village Voice* whether perhaps the concerns of the play were not a consequence of some "personal quirk" of the author. Mr. Novick writes: "But why should Ozzie and Harriet be so obsessively disgusted by David's miscegenation? It seems more the playwright's personal quirk than any kind of meaningful symbol." I would refer him to the fact that upon defeating the French, the North Vietnamese set up rehabilitation programs for the girls who had worked for the French as prostitutes, yet these same North Vietnamese opened that war by issuing orders that all Eurasians be killed and all Vietnamese girls married to Frenchmen or living with them be disemboweled.* Now that's a racism to match the quirk of the play. It also seems an obsessive disgust with miscegenation. Disembowel the source and slaughter the product.

In addition, if Novick had used the word "preoccupation" or "obsession," both of which are more substantial than "quirk," I would, I think, agree with him and then ask: where does he think writing (and particularly playwriting) comes from? In addition, I consider *Sticks and Bones* to be as much about obsession as it is about tribalism—a more inclusive term than "racism"—just as I consider the root of racism to be sex, or more exactly miscegenation.

•   •

Late in the evening on April 23 I sat in my tux in the Broadway Theater, wondering what my face would reveal when *The Prisoner of Second Avenue* was named winner of the 1972 Tony for the Best Play on Broadway. Then I heard Arthur Hill say, "The winner is *Sticks and Bones*," and my wife screamed. Shortly my stunned and stupid look went flashing over television airwaves across the country.

* Bernard Newman, *Background to Viet-Nam* (New York, 1966).

Looking back now, it seems to have been mostly a physical event. Like a basketball player driving for a shot, I had little idea what my hands were doing or whether the expression on my face might be odd. With so little self-awareness, I have almost no memory of the moment and am nagged by a certain curiosity to see a TV tape of the Tonys, as if this electronic version might be a more valid rendition than the sketch my memory offers.

● ●

There was a time when the names Andy, Ginger, Daniel, and Bucky seemed a more aesthetically appropriate choice for the characters in *Sticks and Bones*. I debated the issue within myself and with Joe Papp and Jeff and many others. I cannot say I am totally satisfied with the choice made, though it was my own. There are times when I wonder if a production at some other place and time might try the other set of names. I would be interested to know the effect.

● ●

In the late spring of 1972 the Theater Company of Boston opened a production of *The Basic Training of Pavlo Hummel* starring Al Pacino. Traveling north to see it, I worried over the work they would do upon it, and indeed the production was very different. The activities within each scene were much slower and more naturalistic in development, yet the production's over-all effect was to move deep into a kind of eerie surrealism. Wheeler had worked hard to give the play the sense of an event occurring far within the dying Pavlo's mind. To this end, a hospital bed was a set piece standing in a corner throughout the play. Referred to only occasionally by having Pavlo flee back to its covers, the device of the bed added a brilliant dimension to Pavlo's second-act battlefield woundings. Each time Pavlo was hit, Ardell lifted him and carried him back to the bed. No sooner would Ardell get him into the covers than Pavlo would be up on his feet, dashing for his rifle, getting hit again. Altogether, the Pavlo-Ardell relationship had an interesting awkwardness. Ardell seemed to be forever delivering information either too late for Pavlo's use, or in some way Pavlo could not quite understand. They were out of joint in an inexplicable, interesting, and painful way.

I left the experience very pleased. With subtlety, Al Pacino had delivered the humor, dignity, and baffled cruelty of Pavlo. David Wheeler's production had uncovered reverberations which I had in no way consciously provided for.

●　●

Finally, in my estimation, an "antiwar" play is one that expects, by the very fabric of its executed conception, to have political effect. I anticipated no such consequences from my plays, nor did I conceive them in the hope that they would have such consequences. I have written them to diagnose, as best I can, certain phenomena that went on in and around me. It seems presumptuous and pointless to call them "antiwar" plays. First of all, I believe that to think a play can have immediate, large-scale political effect is to overestimate vastly the power that plays have. In addition, if there is (as I deeply hope there is) more content in these plays than the thin line of political tract, then to categorize them as such is to diminish them. A play in which a family looks bad is not called an "antifamily" play. A play in which a marriage looks bad is not called an "antimarriage" play. A play in which young people seem not the most perfect of beings is not called an "antiyouth" play. A play about criminals is not called an "anticrime" play. I think these labels do not exist because family, marriage, youth, and crime are all viewed as phenomena permanently a part of the eternal human pageant. I believe war to be an equally permanent part of that pageant.

The Basic Training of Pavlo Hummel

For my parents and Joe Papp

CHARACTERS

Pavlo Hummel

Yen

Ardell

Sergeant Tower

Captain (all officers)

Corporal

Kress

Parker

Pierce

Hinkle

Burns

Hendrix

Ryan

Mickey

Mrs. Hummel

Voice of Mrs. Sorrentino

Sergeant Brisbey

Jones

Sergeant Wall

Mamasan

Grennel

Parham

Various soldiers, various Vietnamese

Place and time: The United States Army, 1965–1967

ACT ONE

The set is a space, a platform slanting upward from the down-stage area. The floor is nothing more than slats that run in var-ious directions with a military precision. It has a brownish color. The backdrop is dark with touches of green. Along the back of the set runs a ramp elevated about two feet off the floor. Stage left and a little down from the ramp stands the drill sergeant's tower. This element is stark and as realistic as possible. Farther downstage and stage left the floor opens into a pit two feet deep. There is an old furnace partly visible. Downstage and stage right are three army cots with footlockers at their base. Upstage and stage right there is a bar area: an army ammunition crate and an army oil drum set as a table and chair before a fragment of sheet-metal wall partly covered with beer-can labels. All ele-ments of the set should have some military tone to them, some echo of basic training.

To start the play, pop American music is heard for an instant in the dark. Then lights up on the bar area: evening. A drunken GI sits slumped on the crate, leaning forward on the drum. Yen (pronounced "Ing"), a Vietnamese girl dressed in purple silk pa-jamas—slacks and pullover top—moves about with a beer, trying to settle Pavlo down.

PAVLO, *dressed in fatigues, moving with the music, dealing some-how with the other two in the room as he speaks.* Did I do it to him? The triple-Hummel. Can you hear your boy? (*A sort of shudder runs through his shoulders; he punches.*) A little shuffle and then a triple boom-boom-boom. Ain't I bad, man? Gonna

7

eat up Cleveland. Gonna piss on Chicago. (*Banging with his palms on the sides of the oil drum.*)

YEN. Creezy, creezy.

PAVLO. Dinky dow!

SOLDIER, *disturbed by the banging, looking up, deeply drunk.* Les . . . go . . . home. . . .

YEN. Paablo creezy.

PAVLO. Dinky dow.

YEN. Paablo boocoup love. Sleep me all time . . .

PAVLO. Did I ever tell you?—thirteen months a my life ago— Joanna was her name. Sorrentino, a little bit a guinea-wop made outa all the pins and sticks all bitches are made a. And now I'm the guy who's been with the Aussies. *I had tea with 'em. It was me they called to*—"Hummel!" "MEDIC!" (*With a fairly good Australian accent*) "The dirty little blighters blew me bloody arm off." (*Yen brings a beer.*) Yeh, girl, in a little bit a time. (*And back to the air*) We had a cat, you know? So we had a kitty box, which is a place for the cat to shit.

YEN. Talk "shit." I can talk "shit." Numba-ten talk.

PAVLO. Ohhh, damn that Sorrentino, what she couldn't be taught. And that's what I'd like to do—look her up and explain a few things like, "Your face, Sorrentino, I don't like your ugly face." Did I ever tell you about the ole lady? Did I ever speak her name, me mudda.

YEN. Mudda you, huh, Paablo? Very nice.

PAVLO. To be seen by her now, oh, she would shit her jeans to see me now, up tight with this little odd-lookin' whore, feelin' good, and tall, ready to bed down. Ohhh, Jesus Mahoney. You see what she did, she wrote Joanna a letter. My mother. She called Joanna a dirty little slut, and when I found out, I cried, I wailed, baby, big tears. I screamed and threw kitty litter; I threw it in the air. I screamed over and over, "Happy Birthday, Happy Birthday," and then one day there was Joanna in the subway and she said, "Hello," and told me my favorite jacket I was wearing made me look ugly, didn't fit, made me look fat.

(A grenade, thrown by a hand that merely flashes between the curtains, hits with a loud clump in the room, and everyone looks without moving.)

GRENA-A-ADE!

Pavlo drops to his knees, seizing the grenade, and has it in his hands in his lap when the explosion comes, loud, shattering, and the lights go black, go red or blue. The girl screams. The bodies are strewn about. The radio plays. And a black soldier, Ardell, now appears, his uniform strangely unreal with black ribbons and medals; he wears sunglasses, bloused boots. (Ardell will drift throughout the play, present only when specifically a part of the action, appearing, disappearing, without prominent entrances and exits.) A body detail is also entering, two men with a stretcher to remove the dead.

ARDELL, moving to turn the radio off. You want me, Pavlo? You callin'? Don't I hear you? Yeh, that the way it happen sometimes. Everybody hit, everybody hurtin', but the radio ain't been touched, the dog didn't feel a thing; the engine's good as new but all the people dead and the chassis a wreck, man. (Bowing a little toward Pavlo) Yeh, yeh, some mean motherfucker, you don't even see, blow you away. Don't I hear you callin'? (Pivoting, moving swiftly down center stage) Get off it. Bounce on up here.

Pavlo leaps to his feet, runs to join Ardell.

PAVLO. PFC Pavlo Hummel, Sir. R.A. seven four, three one three, two two six.

ARDELL. We gonna get you your shit straight. No need to call me Sir.

PAVLO. Ardell!

ARDELL. Now what's your unit? Now shout it out.

PAVLO. Second of the Sixteenth, First Division, BIG RED ONE!

ARDELL. Company.

PAVLO. Bravo.

ARDELL. C.O.?

PAVLO. My Company Commander is Captain M. W. Henderson. My Battalion Commander is Lieutenant Colonel Roy J. S. Tully.

ARDELL. Platoon?

PAVLO. Third.

ARDELL. Squad.

PAVLO. Third.

ARDELL. Squad and platoon leaders.

PAVLO. My platoon leader is First Lieutenant David R. Barnes; my squad leader is Staff Sergeant Peter T. Collins.

ARDELL. You got family?

PAVLO. No.

ARDELL. You lyin', Boy.

PAVLO. One mother; one half brother.

ARDELL. All right.

PAVLO. Yes.

ARDELL. Soldier, what you think a the war?

PAVLO. It's being fought.

ARDELL. Ain't no doubt about that.

PAVLO. No.

ARDELL. You kill anybody?

PAVLO. Yes.

ARDELL. Like it?

PAVLO. Yes.

ARDELL. Have nightmares?

PAVLO. Pardon?

ARDELL. What we talkin' about, Boy?

PAVLO. No.

ARDELL. How tall you? you lyin' motherfucker.

PAVLO. Five-ten.

ARDELL. Eyes.

PAVLO. Green.

ARDELL. Hair.

PAVLO. Red.

ARDELL. Weight.

PAVLO. One-five-two.

ARDELL. What you get hit with?

PAVLO. Hand grenade. Fragmentation-type.

ARDELL. Where about it get you?

PAVLO, *touching gently his stomach and crotch.* Here. And here. Mostly in the abdominal and groin areas.

ARDELL. Who you talkin' to? Don't you talk that shit to me, man. Abdominal and groin areas, that shit. It hit you in the stomach, man, like a ten-ton truck and it hit you in the balls, blew 'em away. Am I lyin'?

PAVLO, *able to grin: glad to grin.* No, man.

ARDELL. Hurt you bad.

PAVLO. Killed me.

ARDELL. That right. Made you dead. You dead man; how you feel about that?

PAVLO. Well . . .

ARDELL. *Don't you know? I think you know!* I think it piss you off. I think you lyin' you say it don't. Make you wanna scream.

PAVLO. Yes.

ARDELL. You had that thing in your hand, didn't you? What was you thinkin' on, you had that thing in your hand?

PAVLO. About throwin' it. About a man I saw when I was eight years old who came through the neighborhood with a softball team called the Demons, and he could do anything with a softball underhand that most big-leaguers could do with a hardball overhand. He was fantastic.

ARDELL. That all?

Gramley Library
Salem College
Winston-Salem, NC 27108

PAVLO. Yes.

ARDELL. You ain't lyin'.

PAVLO. No.

A whistle blows loudly and figures run about behind Pavlo and Ardell, a large group of men in fatigues without markings other than their name tags and U.S. Army. And on the high drill instructor's tower, which is dimly lit at the moment, stands a large Negro Sergeant. A captain observes from the distance. A corporal prowls among the gathering troopers, checking buttons, etc.

PAVLO, *looking about.* Who're they?

ARDELL. Man, don't you jive me. You know who they are. That Fort Gordon, man. They Echo Company, Eighth Battalion, Third Training Regiment. They basic training, baby.

PAVLO—*removes PFC stripes and 1st Division patch.* Am I . . . really . . . dead . . . ?

ARDELL. Damn near, man; real soon. Comin' on. Eight more weeks. Got wings as big as streets. Got large, large wings.

PAVLO. It happened . . . to me. . . .

ARDELL. Whatever you say, Pavlo.

PAVLO. Sure . . . that grenade come flyin', I caught it, held it.

Pause.

ARDELL. New York, huh?

PAVLO. Manhattan. Two thirty-one East Forty-fifth. I—

ARDELL. Now we know who we talkin' about. Somebody say "Pavlo Hummel," we know who they mean.

SGT. TOWER. GEN'LMEN! *(As the men standing in ranks below the tower snap to parade rest and Pavlo, startled, runs to find his place among them)* You all lookin' up here and can you see me? Can you see me well? Can you hear and comprehend my words? Can you see what is written here? Over my right tit-tee, can you read it? Tower. My name. And I am bigger than my name. And can you see what is sewn here upon the muscle of my arm? Can you see it? ANSWER!

THE MEN—*yell.* NO.

SGT. TOWER. No, what? WHAT?

THE MEN. NO, SERGEANT.

SGT. TOWER. It is also my name. It is my first name. *Sergeant.* That who I am. I you Field First. And you gonna see a lot a me. You gonna see so much a me, let me tell you, you gonna think I you mother, father, sisters, brothers, aunts, uncles, nephews, nieces, and children—if-you-got-'em—all rolled into one big black man. Yeh, Gen'lmen. And you gonna become me. You gonna learn to stand tall and be proud and you gonna run as far and shoot as good. Or else you gonna be ashamed; I am one old man and you can't outdo no thirty-eight-year-old man, you ashamed. AM I GONNA MAKE YOU ASHAMED? WHAT DO YOU SAY?

THE MEN. Yes, Sergeant!

SGT. TOWER. NO! NO, GEN'LMEN. No, I am not gonna make you ashamed. SERGEANT, YOU ARE NOT GONNA MAKE US ASHAMED.

THE MEN. SERGEANT, YOU ARE NOT GONNA MAKE US ASHAMED.

SGT. TOWER. WE ARE GONNA DO EVERYTHING YOU CAN DO AND DO YOU ONE BETTER!

THE MEN. WE ARE GONNA DO EVERYTHING YOU CAN DO AND DO YOU ONE BETTER!

SGT. TOWER. YOU A BUNCH A LIARS. YOU A BUNCH A FOOLS! Now you listen up; you listen to me. No one does me one better. And especially no people like you. Don't you know what you are? *Trainees!* And there ain't nothin' lower on this earth except for one thing, and we all know what that is, do we not, Gen'lmen?

THE MEN. *Yes* . . . Sergeant. . . .

SGT. TOWER. And what is that? (*Pause.*) And you told me you knew! Did you lie to me? Oh, no, nooo, I can't believe that; please, please, don't lie. Gen'lmen, did you lie?

THE MEN—*they are sorry.* Yes, Sergeant.

SGT. TOWER. No, no, please. If there something you don't know, you tell me. If I ask you something and you do not know the answer, let me know. Civilians. That the answer to my question. The only creatures in this world lower than trainees is civilians, and we hate them all. All. (*Quick pause.*) And now . . . and finally . . . and most important, do you see what is written here? Over my heart; over my left tit-tee, do you see? U.S. Army. Which is where I live. Which is where we all live. Can you, Gen'lmen, can you tell me you first name now, do you know it? (*Quick pause as he looks about in dismay.*) Don't you know? I think you do, yes, I do, but you just too shy to say it. Like little girls watchin' that thing just get bigger and bigger for the first time, you shy. And what did I tell you to do when you don't know the answer I have asked?

THE MEN. What is our first name?

SGT. TOWER. You! You there! (*Suddenly pointing into the ranks of men*) You! Ugly! Yeah, you. That right. You ugly. Ain't you. YOU TAKE ONE BIG STEP FORWARD.

(*And it is Pavlo stepping hesitantly forward. He does not know what he has done or what is expected from him.*)

I think I saw you were not in harmony with the rest of these men. I think I saw that you were looking about at the air like some kinda fool and that malingering, Trainee, and that intol'able. So you drop, you hear me. You drop down on your ugly little hands and knees and lift up you butt and knees from off that beautiful Georgia clay and you give me TEN and that's push-ups of which I am speaking.

(*Pavlo, having obeyed the orders step by step, now begins the push-ups. Tower goes back to the men.*)

NOW YOU ARE TRAINEES, ALL YOU PEOPLE, AND YOU LISTEN UP. I ASK YOU WHAT IS YOUR FIRST NAMES, YOU TELL ME "TRAINEES"!

THE MEN—*yell.* TRAINEE!

SGT. TOWER. TRAINEE, SERGEANT!

THE MEN. TRAINEE, SERGE—

SGT. TOWER. I CAN'T HEAR YOU!

THE MEN. *TRAINEE, SERGEANT!*

SGT. TOWER. AND WHAT IS YOUR LAST NAMES? YOU OWN LAST FUCKING NAMES?

THE MEN. (*A chorus of American names.*)

SGT. TOWER. AND YOU LIVE IN THE ARMY OF THE UNITED STATES OF AMERICA.

THE MEN. AND WE LIVE IN THE ARMY OF THE UNITED STATES OF AMERICA.

SGT. TOWER. WITH BALLS BETWEEN YOU LEGS! YOU HAVE BALLS! NO SLITS! BUT BALLS, AND YOU—

Having risen, Pavlo is getting back into ranks.

THE MEN. AND WE HAVE BALLS BETWEEN OUR LEGS! NO SLITS, BUT BALLS!

SGT. TOWER, *suddenly back at Pavlo.* UGLY! Now who tole you to stand? Who you think you are, you standin', nobody tole you to stand. You drop. You drop, you hear me.

(*And Pavlo goes back into the push-up position.*)

What your name, Boy?

PAVLO. Yes, Sir.

SGT. TOWER. Your name, Boy!

PAVLO. Trainee Hummel, Sir!

SGT. TOWER. Sergeant.

PAVLO. Yes, Sir.

SGT. TOWER. Sergeant. I AM A SERGEANT!

PAVLO. SERGEANT. YOU ARE A SERGEANT!

SGT. TOWER. All right. That nice; all right, only in the future, you doin' push-ups, I want you countin' and that countin' so loud it scare me so I think there some kinda terrible, terrible man comin' to get me. Am I understood?

PAVLO. Yes, Sergeant.

SGT. TOWER. I can't hear you!

PAVLO. Yes, Sergeant! Yes, Sergeant!

SGT. TOWER. All right! You get up and fall back where you was. Gen'lmen. You are gonna fall out. By platoon. Which is how you gonna be doin' most everything from now on—by platoon and by the numbers—includin' takin' a shit. Somebody say to you, "One!" you down; "two!" you doin' it; "three!" you wipin' and you ain't finished, you cuttin' it off. I CAN'T HEAR YOU!

THE MEN. YES, SERGEANT.

SGT. TOWER. I say to you "squat!" and you all hunkered down and got nothin' to say to anybody but "How much?" and "What color, Sergeant?"

THE MEN. Yes, Sergeant.

SGT. TOWER. You good people. You a good group. Now I gonna call you to attention and you gonna snap to. That's heels on a line or as near it as the conformation of your body permit; head up, chin in, knees not locked; you relaxed. Am I understood?

THE MEN. Yes—

SGT. TOWER. AM I UNDERSTOOD, GODDAMNIT, OR DO YOU WANT TO ALL DROP FOR TWENTY OR—

Ardell, off to the side, is drifting nearer.

THE MEN. YES, SERGEANT, YES, SERGEANT!

ARDELL. Pavlo, my man, you on your way!

CORPORAL. PLATOOOON! PLATOOOON!

SGT. TOWER. I GONNA DO SOME SINGIN', GEN'LMEN, I WANT IT COMIN' BACK TO ME LIKE WE IN GRAND CANYON—

CORPORAL. TEN–HUT!

ARDELL. DO IT, GET IT!

SGT. TOWER. —AND YOU MY MOTHERFUCKIN' ECHO!

SQUAD LEADERS. RIGHT FACE!

Ardell and Pavlo

CORPORAL. FORWARD HARCH!

SGT. TOWER, *singing*. LIFT YOUR HEAD AND LIFT IT HIGH . . .

THE MEN. LIFT YOUR HEAD AND LIFT IT HIGH . . .

SGT. TOWER. ECHO COMPANY PASSIN' BY!

THE MEN. ECHO COMPANY PASSIN' BY!

They start going off in groups, marching and singing.

ARDELL. MOTHER, MOTHER, WHAT'D I DO?

THE MEN. MOTHER, MOTHER, WHAT'D I DO?

ARDELL. THIS ARMY TREATIN' ME WORSE THAN YOU!

THE MEN. THIS ARMY TREATIN' ME WORSE THAN YOU!

SGT. TOWER. LORD HAVE MERCY I'M SO BLUE!

THE MEN. LORD HAVE MERCY I'M SO BLUE! IT EIGHT MORE WEEKS TILL WE BE THROUGH! IT EIGHT MORE WEEKS TILL WE BE THROUGH! IT EIGHT MORE WEEKS TILL WE BE THROUGH!

And all the men have marched off in lines in different directions, giving a sense of large numbers, a larger space, and now, out of this movement, comes a spin-off of two men, Kress and Parker, drilling down the center of the stage, yelling the last of the song, marching stomping, then breaking and running stage left and into the furnace room, where there is the hulk of the belly of the furnace, the flickering of the fire. Kress is large, muscular, with a constant manner of small confusion as if he feels always that something is going on that he nearly, but not quite, understands. Yet there is something seemingly friendly about him. Parker is smaller; he wears glasses.

KRESS. I can't stand it, Parker, bein' so cold all the time and they're all insane, Parker. Waxin' and buffin' the floor at five-thirty in the morning is insane. And then you can't eat till you go down the monkey bars and you gotta eat in ten minutes and can't talk to nobody, and no place in Georgia is warm. I'm from Jersey. I can jump up in the air, if there's a good wind, I'll land in Fort

Dix. Am I right so far? So Sam gets me. What's he do? Fort Dix? Uh-uh. Fort Gordon, Georgia. So I can be warm right? Down South, man. Daffodils and daisies. Year round. *(Hollering)* BUT AM I WARM? DO YOU THINK I'M WARM? DO I LOOK LIKE I'M WARM? JESUS H! EVEN IN THE GODDAMN FURNACE ROOM, I'M FREEZIN' TA DEATH!

PARKER. So, what the hell is hollerin' like a stupid ape gonna do except to let 'em know where we're at?

KRESS *(as Pavlo enters upstage, moving slowly in awe toward the tower, looking).* Heat up my blood!

ARDELL, *to Pavlo.* What you doin' strollin' about like a fool, man? You gonna have people comin' down all over you, don't you know—

OFFICER, *having just entered.* What're you doin' walkin' in this company area? Don't you know you run in this company area? Hummel, you drop, you hear me. You drop!

Pavlo drops and begins the push-ups.

ARDELL, *over him.* Do 'em right, do 'em right!

KRESS. Why can't I be warm? I wanna be warm.

PARKER. Okay, man, you're warm.

KRESS. No; I'm not; I'm cold, Parker. Where's our goddamn fireman; don't he ever do nothin' but push-ups? Don't he ever do nothin' but trouble!

PARKER. Don't knock that ole boy, Kress; I'm tellin' you Hummel's gonna keep us laughin'!

KRESS. Yesterday I was laughin' so hard. I mean, I'm stupid, Parker, but Hummel's *stupid.* I mean, he volunteers to be fireman 'cause he thinks it means you ride in a raincoat on a big red truck and when there's nothin' to do you play cards.

PARKER. Yeah! He don't know it means you gotta baby-sit the goddamn furnace all night, every night. And end up lookin' like a stupid chimney sweep!

KRESS. Lookin' what?

PARKER *(as Pierce enters at a jog, moving across the stage toward Ardell and Pavlo).* Like a goddamn chimney sweep!

PAVLO. Where you goin'?

PIERCE, *without hesitating.* Weapons room and furnace room.

PAVLO, *getting to his feet.* Can I come along?

PIERCE, *still running, without looking back.* I don't give a shit.

He exits, Pavlo following, as Ardell is drifting the opposite direction.

PAVLO. . . . great . . .

KRESS. Yeh? Yeh, Parker, that's good. Chimney sweeps!

PARKER. Yeh, they were these weird little men always crawlin' around, and they used to do this weird shit ta chimneys.

Pierce and Pavlo enter. They have their rifles. Pierce is a trainee acting as a squad leader. He has a cloth marked with corporal's stripes tied on his left sleeve.

PIERCE. At ease!

KRESS. Hey, the Chimney Shit. Hey, what's happenin', Chimney Shit?

PAVLO. How you doin', Kress?

KRESS. Where's your red hat, man?

PAVLO. What?

PARKER. Ain't you got no red fireman's hat?

PAVLO. I'm just with Pierce, that's all. He's my squad leader and I'm with him.

PARKER. Mr. Squad Leader.

PAVLO. Isn't that right, Pierce?

PARKER. Whose ass you kiss to get that job, anyway, Pierce?

PIERCE. At ease, Trainees.

KRESS. He's R.A., man. Regular Army. Him and Hummel. Lifer morons. Whata they gonna do to us today, anyway, Mr. Actin'

Sergeant, Corporal. What's the lesson for the day: first aid or bayonet? I love this fuckin' army.

PIERCE. The schedule's posted, Kress!

KRESS. You know I don't read, man; hurts my eyes; makes 'em water.

PAVLO. When's the gas chamber, that's what I wanna know.

KRESS. For you, Chimney Shit, in about ten seconds when I fart in your face.

PAVLO. I'm all right. I do all right.

KRESS. Sure you do, except you got your head up your ass.

PAVLO. Yeh? Well maybe I'd rather have it up my ass than where you got it.

Slight pause: it has made no sense to Kress at all.

KRESS. What?

PAVLO. You heard me, Kress.

KRESS. What'd he say, Parker? *(There is frenzy in this.)* I heard him, but I don't know what he said. WHAT'D YOU SAY TO ME, HUMMEL?

PAVLO. Just never you mind, Kress.

KRESS. I DON'T KNOW WHAT YOU SAID TO ME, YOU WEIRD PERSON!

PARKER, *patting Kress.* Easy, man, easy; be cool.

KRESS. But I don't like weird people, Parker. I don't like them. How come I gotta be around him? I don't wanna be around you, Hummel!

PAVLO. Don't you worry about it, I'm just here with Pierce. I just wanna know about the gas chamber.

KRESS. It's got gas in it! Ain't that right, Parker! It's like this goddamn giant asshole, it farts on you. THHPPBBBZZZZZZZZ!

Silence.

PAVLO. When is it, Pierce?

KRESS. Ohhhhh, Jesus, I'm cold.

PAVLO. This ain't cold, Kress.

KRESS. I know if I'm cold.

PAVLO. I been colder than this. This ain't cold. I been a lot colder than—

KRESS. DON'T TELL ME IT AIN'T COLD OR I'LL KILL YOU! JESUS GOD ALMIGHTY I HATE THIS MOTHER ARMY STICKIN' ME IN WITH WEIRD PEOPLE! DIE, HUMMEL! Will you please do me that favor! Oh, God, let me close my eyes and when I open them, Hummel is dead. Please. Please.

He squeezes his eyes shut, clenches his hands and then looks at Pavlo, who is grinning.

PAVLO. Boy, I sure do dread that gas chamber.

KRESS. He hates me, Parker. He truly hates me.

PAVLO. No, I don't.

KRESS. What'd I ever do to him, you suppose.

PARKER. I don't know, Kress.

PAVLO. I don't hate you.

PARKER. How come he's so worried about that gas chamber, that's what I wonder.

PAVLO. Well, see, I had an uncle die in San Quentin.

(Kress screams.)

That's the truth, Kress.

(Kress screams again.)

I don't care if you believe it. He killed four people in a fight in a bar.

PARKER. Usin' his bare hands, right?

PAVLO. You know how many people are executed every damn day in San Quentin? One hell of a lot. And every one of 'em just about is somebody's uncle and one of 'em was my Uncle Roy. He killed four people in a barroom brawl usin' broken bottles and table legs and screamin', jus' screamin'. He was mean, man.

He was rotten; and my folks been scared the same thing might happen to me; all their lives, they been scared. I got that same look in my eyes like him.

PARKER. What kinda look is that?

KRESS. That really rotten look, man. He got that really rotten look. Can't you see it?

PAVLO. You ever steal a car, Kress? You know how many cars I stole?

KRESS. Shut up Hummel! You're a goddamn chimney sweep and I don't wanna talk to you because you don't talk American, you talk Hummel! Some goddamn foreign language!

PARKER. How many cars you stole?

PAVLO. Twenty-three.

KRESS. Twenty-three!

Parker whistles.

PAVLO. That's a lotta cars, huh?

PARKER. You damn betcha, man. How long'd it take you, for chrissake? Ten years?

PAVLO. Two.

PARKER. Workin' off and on, you mean.

PAVLO. Sure. Not every night, or they'd catch you. And not always from the same part of town. Man, sometimes I'd hit lower Manhattan, and then the next night the Bronx or Queens, and sometimes I'd even cut right out outa town. One time, in fact, I went all the way to New Haven. Boy that was some night because they almost caught me. Can you imagine that. Huh? Parker? Huh? Pierce? All the way to New Haven and cops on my tail every inch a the way, roadblocks closin' up behind me, bang, bang, and then some highway patrolman, just as I was wheelin' into New Haven, he come roarin' outa this side road. See, they must a called ahead or somethin' and he come hot on my ass. I kicked it, man, arrrrgggggghhhhh . . . ! Eighty-two per. Had a Porsche; he didn't know who he was after; that stupid fuzz, eighty-two per, straight down the gut, people jumpin' outa my way, kids and businessmen and little old ladies, all of 'em, and me kickin' ass, up to ninety-seven now, roarin' baby sirens all around me, so I cut into this alley and jump. Oh, Jesus, Christ, just lettin' the car go, I hit, roll, I'm up and runnin' down for this board fence, up and over, sirens all over now, I mean, *all over*, but I'm walkin' calm, I'm cool. Cops are goin' this way and that way. One of 'em asks me if I seen a Porsche go by real fast. Did *I* see—

KRESS. *Jesus-goddamn*—the furnace room's smellin' like the gas chamber!

He rises to leave, Parker following.

PARKER. Right, Hummel. That's right. I mean I liked your story about your really rotten uncle Roy better than the one about all the cars.

KRESS. Gotta go get our weapons.

PARKER. Defend our fuckin' selves.

PAVLO. I'll see you guys later.

(They are gone. Silence.)

Hey Pierce, you wanna hear my General Orders; make sure I know 'em, okay? Like we're on guard mount and you're the O.D. . . . You wanna see if I'm sharp enough to be one a your boys. Okay? *(Snapping to attention)* Sir! My first general order is to take charge of this post and all government property in view, keeping always on the alert and . . .

PIERCE. Gimme your eighth, Hummel.

PAVLO. Eighth? No, no, lemme do 'em one, two, three. You'll mess me up I don't do them one, two, three.

PIERCE. That's the way it's gonna be, Hummel. The man comes up to you on guard mount he's gonna be all over you—right on top a you yellin' down your throat. You understand me? He won't be standin' back polite and pretty lettin' you run your mouth.

PAVLO. Just to practice, Pierce. I just wanna practice.

PIERCE. You don't wanna practice shit. You just wanna stand there and have me pat your goddamned head for bein' a good boy. Don't you know we stood here laughin' at you lyin' outa your ass? Don't you have any pride, man?

PAVLO. I got pride. And anyway, they didn't know I was lyin'.

PIERCE. Shit.

PAVLO. And anyway, I wasn't lyin'; it was story telling. They was just messin' with me a little, pickin' on me. My mom used to always tell my dad not to be so hard on me, but he knew.

Whistle blows loudly from off.

PIERCE. Let's go.

PAVLO. See, he was hard on me 'cause he loved me. I'm R.A. Pierce.

PIERCE. You got an R.A. prefix, man, but you ain't Regular Army.

PAVLO. They was just jumpin' on me a little; pickin' on me.

Again the whistle.

PIERCE. That whistle means formation, man.

PAVLO. They're just gonna draw weapons and I already got mine.

PIERCE. That ain't what I said, Jerkoff!

PAVLO. Well, I ain't goin' out there to stand around doin' nothin' when I can stay right here and put the time to good use practicin' D and D.

Again the whistle. The men are gathering; we hear their murmuring.

PIERCE. You ain't no motherin' exception to that whistle!

PAVLO. You ain't any real corporal anyway, Pierce. So don't get so big with me just because you got that hunk a thing wrapped around you—

PIERCE. Don't you mess up my squad, Hummel! Don't you make me look bad or I'll get you your legs broken.

PAVLO (*as whistle blows and Pierce is running and gone*). I bet you never heard a individual initiative.

Whistle again as soldiers rush in to line up in formation at parade rest while Sgt. Tower climbs to stand atop the platform.

ARDELL. They don't know, do they? They don't know who they talkin' to.

PAVLO. No.

ARDELL. You gonna be so straight.

PAVLO. So clean.

(As Sgt. Tower, noticing that someone is missing from formation, turns, descends, exits.)

Port Harms!

And he does the move with only a slight and quickly corrected error.

ARDELL. Good, Pavlo. Good. *(Slight pause.)* Order Harms!

There is some skill in the move.

PAVLO. Okay . . .

ARDELL. RIGHT SHOULDER . . . HARMS!

Pavlo's head flinches, the rifle nicking the top of his helmet. His back is toward the group. Sgt. Tower enters, watches for a time.

PAVLO. Goddamnit. Shit.

Again the rifle back to order arms.

ARDELL. RIGHT SHOULDER . . .

PAVLO. HARMS!

(Again it is not good.)

You mother rifle. You stupid fucking rifle. RIGHT SHOULDER, HARMS. *(He tries.)* Mother! Stupid mother, whatsamatter with you? I'll kill you! *(And he has it high above his head. He is looking up.)* Rifle, please. Work for me, do it for me. I know what to do, just do it.

ARDELL. Just go easy. Man . . . just easy. It don't mean that much. What's it matter?

SGT. TOWER. What you doin', Trainee?

PAVLO, *snapping to attention.* Yes, Sir! Trainee Pavlo Hummel, Sir.

SGT. TOWER. I didn't ask you you name, Boy. I asked you what you doin' in here when you supposed to be out on that formation?

PAVLO. Yes, Sir.

SGT. TOWER. No, I don't have no bars on my collar; do you see any bars on my collar?

PAVLO, *looking.* No . . . No . . .

SGT. TOWER. But what do you see on my sleeve at about the height a my shoulder less a little, what do you see?

PAVLO. Stripes, Sergeant. Sergeant stripes.

SGT. TOWER. So how come you call me Sir? I ain't no Sir. I don't want to be no Sir. I am a Sergeant. Now do we know one another?

PAVLO. Yes, Sergeant.

SGT. TOWER. That mean you can answer my question in the proper manner, do it not?

PAVLO. I was practicin' D and D, Sergeant, to make me a good soldier.

SGT. TOWER. Ohhhhhhh! I think you tryin' to jive this ole man, that what you doin'. Or else you awful stupid, because all the good soldiers is out there in that formation like they supposed to when they hear that whistle. Now which?

PAVLO. Pardon, Sergeant?

SGT. TOWER. Which is it? You jivin' on me or you awful stupid, you take your pick. And lemme tell you why you can't put no jive on the old Sarge. Because long time ago, this ole Sarge was one brand-new, baby-soft, smart-assed recruit. So I see you and I say, "What that young recruit doin' in that furnace room this whole company out there bein' talked at by the C.O.?" And the answer come to me like a blast a thunder and this voice sayin' to me in my head, "This here young recruit jerkin' off, that what he doin'," and then into my head come this picture and we ain't in no furnace room, we in that jungle catchin' hell from this one little yellow man and his automatic weapon that he chained to up on top of this hill. "Get on up that hill!" I tell my young recruit.

And he tell me, "Yes, Sergeant," like he been taught, and then he start thinkin' to hisself, "What that ole Sarge talkin' about, 'run on up that hill'? Ah git my ass blown clean away. I think maybe he got hit on his head, he don't know what he talkin' about no more—maybe I go on over behind that ole rock—practice me a little D and D." Ain't that some shit the way them young recruits wanna carry on? So what I think we do, you and me, long about twenty-two hundred hours we do a little D and D and PT and all them kinda alphabetical things. Make you a good soldier.

PAVLO, *thinking he wants to work with Sgt. Tower.* I don't think I can. That's nighttime, Sergeant, and I'm a fireman. I got to watch the furnace.

SGT. TOWER. That don't make me no never mind. We jus' work it in between your shifts. You see? Ain't it a wonder how you let the old Sarge do the worryin' and figurin' and he find a way?

(Turns, starting to leave.)

PAVLO. Sergeant, I was wondering how many push-ups you can do. How many you can do, that's how many I want to be able to do before I ever leave.

SGT. TOWER. Boy, don't you go sayin' no shit like that, you won't ever get out. You be an ole bearded blind fuckin' man pushin' up all over Georgia.

Sgt. Tower moves to leave, and Pavlo, speaking immediately and rapidly, in a single rush of breath, again stops him. Incredulously Sgt. Tower watches, starts to leave, watches.

PAVLO. And I was wondering also, Sergeant Tower, and wanted to ask you—when I was leaving home, my mother wanted to come along to the train station, but I lied to her about the time. She would have wanted to hug me right in front of everybody. She would have waved a handkerchief at the train. It would have been awful.

(Sgt. Tower turns; now he is leaving.)

She would have stood there waving. Was I wrong?

CORPORAL. TEN–HUT! FORWARD HARCH!

*And the men begin to march in place, while Pavlo, without join-
ing them, also marches.*

SGT. TOWER.   AIN'T NO USE IN GOIN' HOME.

THE MEN, *beginning to exit.* AIN'T NO USE IN GOIN' HOME.

SGT. TOWER, *at the side of the stage.* JODY GOT YOUR GAL
AND GONE.

THE MEN.   JODY HUMPIN' ON AND ON.

SGT. TOWER.   AIN'T NO USE IN GOIN' BACK.

And Pavlo, in his own area, is marching away.

THE MEN.   JODY GOT OUR CADILLAC.

CORPORAL.   AIN'T NO MATTER WHAT WE DO.

ALL.   JODY DOIN' OUR SISTER TOO.

CORPORAL.   Count cadence, delayed cadence, count cadence, count!

ALL.   One— two— three— four— One, two, three, four. One, two,
three, four. *Hey!*

*All are now gone except Pavlo, who spins out of his marching
pattern to come stomping to a halt in the furnace-room area,
while Ardell drifts toward him.*

ARDELL.   Oh, yeh; army train you, shape you up, teach you all kinds
a good stuff. Like Bayonet. It all about what you do you got no
more bullets and this man after you. So you put this knife on the
end a your rifle, start yellin' and carryin' on. Then there Hand to
Hand. Hand to Hand cool.

(Pavlo is watching, listening.)

It all about hittin' and kickin'. What you do when you got no
gun and no knife. Then there CBR. CBR: Chemical, Biological,
and Radiological Warfare. What you do when some mean motherfucker hit you with some kinda chemical. You

(Ardell mimes throwing a grenade at Pavlo.)

got green fuckin' killin' smoke all around you. What you gonna
do? You gotta git on your protective mask. You ain't got it?

PAVLO, *choking.* But I'm too beautiful to die. (*Rummages about in the furnace room.*)

ARDELL, *throwing a mask to him.* But you the only one who believe that, Pavlo. You gotta be hollerin' loud as you know how, "Gas!" And then, sweet lord almighty, little bit later, you walkin' along, somebody else hit you with some kinda biological jive. But you know your shit. Mask on.

And Pavlo, having put the mask on, is waving his arms.

PAVLO. GAS! GAS! GAS!

ARDELL. You gettin' it, Pavlo. All right. Lookin' real good. But now you tired and you still walkin' and you come up on somebody bad—this boy mean—he hit you with radiation.

Pavlo goes into a tense, defensive posture.

PAVLO, *realizing his helplessness.* Awww.

ARDELL. That right. You know what you do? You kinda stand there, that what you do, whimperin' and talkin' to yourself, 'cause he got you. You gotta be some kinda fool, somebody hit you with radiation, man, you put on a mask, start hollerin', "Gas." Am I lyin'? Pavlo. What do you say?

PAVLO. Aww, no. . . . No man— No, No— No, no. No, no. Oh . . .

(*There has been, toward the end of this, a gathering of a group of soldiers in the barracks area. Pavlo, muttering in denial of the radiation, crosses the stage hurriedly, fleeing the radiation, and runs into Parker, who grabs him, spins him.*)

I did not.

KRESS. The hell you didn't.

PARKER, *kneeling behind Pavlo to take a billfold from his pocket.* You been found out, Jerkoff.

PAVLO. No.

KRESS. We got people saw you. Straight honest guys.

PARKER. Get that thing (*meaning the mask*) off your face.

BURNS. The shit I didn't see you.

PARKER. You never saw a billfold before in your life, is that what you're tryin' to say? You didn't even know what it was?

KRESS. Is that what you're tryin' to say, Hummel?

PAVLO. No.

KRESS. What are you tryin' to say?

PAVLO. I'm goin' to bed. (*Moves toward his bed but is stopped by Kress.*)

KRESS. We already had two guys lose money to some thief around here, Shitbird, and we got people sayin' they saw you with Hinkle's billfold in your pudgy little paws.

HINKLE, *in a deep Southern drawl (as Parker hands him the billfold he found on Pavlo)*. Is that right, Hummel?

PAVLO. I was just testin' you, Hinkle, to see how stupid you were leavin' your billfold layin' out like that when somebody's been stealin' right in our own platoon. What kinda army is this anyway, you're supposed to trust people with your life, you can't even trust 'em not to steal your money.

PARKER. Listen to him.

PAVLO. That's the truth, Parker. I was just makin' a little test experiment to see how long it'd be before he'd notice it was gone. I don't steal.

KRESS. What about all them cars?

PAVLO. What cars?

PARKER. The New Haven Caper, Jerkoff. You know.

PAVLO. Ohhh, that was different, you guys. That was altogether different.

KRESS. Yeh, they were cars and you couldn't fit them in your pocket.

PAVLO. Those people weren't my friends.

PARKER. You don't steal from your friends. That what you're sayin'? Kress, Hummel says he don't steal from his friends.

KRESS, *jumping up on Pavlo's bed, standing, walking about.* Don't that make his prospects pretty damn near unlimited.

PAVLO. Hey! Kress; what're you doin'?

KRESS. What?

PAVLO. I said, "What're you up to?" You're on my bed.

KRESS. Who is?

PAVLO. You are. You are.

KRESS. Where?

PAVLO. Right here. You're on my bed. That's my bed.

KRESS. No it isn't. It's not anybody's. It's not yours, Hummel.

PAVLO. It is too.

KRESS. Did you buy it?

PAVLO. Get off my bed, Kress!

KRESS. If you didn't buy it, then how is it yours, Ugly!

PAVLO. It was given to me.

KRESS. By who?

PAVLO. You know by who, Kress. The army gave it to me. Get off it.

KRESS. Are you going to take it with you when you leave here? If it's yours, you ought to be planning on taking it with you; are you?

PAVLO. I can't do that.

KRESS. You're taking people's billfolds; you're taking their money; why can't you take this bed?

PAVLO. Because it was just loaned to me.

KRESS. Do you have any kind of papers to prove that? Do you have papers to prove that this is your bed?

PAVLO. There's proof in the orderly room; in the orderly room, or maybe the supply room and you know it. That bed's got a number on it somewhere and that number is like its name and that name is by my name on some papers somewhere in the supply room or the orderly room.

KRESS. Go get them.

PAVLO. What do you mean?

KRESS. Go get them. Bring them here.

PAVLO. I can't.

KRESS. If they're yours, you can.

PAVLO. They're not my papers, it's my bed. Get off my bed, Kress.

(*Kress kneels, taking a more total possession of the bed.*)

Goddamnit, Kress. GODDAMNIT!

(*Silence as Kress seems in fact about to lie down.*)

All right. Okay. You sleep in my bed, I'm gonna sleep in yours.

Pavlo charges toward Kress's bed. Kress rises a little, tense, as all stand watching Pavlo.

KRESS. No, Hummel.

PAVLO, *yelling.* The hell I ain't, Kress.

KRESS. No, no, I strongly advise against it. I do strongly so advise. Or something awful might happen. I might get up in the middle of the night to take a leak and stagger back to my old bed. Lord knows what I might think you are . . . laying there. Lord knows what I might do.

PAVLO, *yelling.* Then get out of my bed.

KRESS. You don't understand at all, do you, Shitbird! I'm sleeping here. This is where I'm going to sleep. You're not going to sleep anywhere. You're going to sit up, or sleep on the floor, whatever. And in the morning, you're going to make this bed. This one. Because if you don't, it'll be unmade when Sergeant Tower comes to inspect in the morning and, as we've already discussed, there's papers somewhere in one room or another and they show whose bed this is.

PAVLO, *rushing back, stomping, raging.* GODDAMN YOU, KRESS, GET OUT OF MY BED! GET OFF MY BED! GET OUT OF IT!

Whistle blows and everyone scrambles. There is the popping of many rifles firing as on the ramp across the back three or four men are in firing position; others stand behind them at port arms until Sgt. Tower calls, "Cease fire!" and the firing stops. The men who have been firing put their rifles on their shoulders to be cleared. Sgt. Tower walks behind them, tapping each on the head when he has seen the weapon is clear. The men leap to their feet. Sgt. Tower then steps out in front of them, begins to pace up and down.

SGT. TOWER. GEN'LMEN! IT GETTIN' TOWARD DARK NOW AND WE GOT TO GET HOME. IT A LONG LONG WAYS TO HOME AND OUR MOTHERS GOT SUPPER READY WAITIN' FOR US. WHAT CAN WE DO? WE GOT TO GET HOME FAST AS WE CAN, WHAT CAN WE DO? DO ANYBODY HAVE AN IDEA? LET ME HEAR YOU SPEAK IF YOU DO. . . . I HAVE AN IDEA. ANYBODY KNOW MY IDEA, LET ME HEAR IF YOU DO.

PAVLO. Run . . .

BURNS. Run?

SGT. TOWER. WHAT?

MORE MEN. RUN!

SGT. TOWER. I CAN'T HEAR YOU.

THE MEN. WHAT?

SGT. TOWER. RUN!

THE MEN. RUN!

SGT. TOWER and THE MEN. RUN! RUN! RUN! RUN! RUN!

SGT. TOWER (*as the men still yell,* "Run, run"). PORT HARMS . . . WHOOO! DOUBLE TIME . . . WHOOOOO!

(*They have been running in place. Now Sgt. Tower leads them off. They exit, running, reappear, exit, and reappear, spreading out now, though Pavlo is fairly close behind Sgt. Tower, who enters once again to run to a point downstage, where he turns to Pavlo entering staggering, leading.*)

FALL OUT!

And Pavlo collapses. The others struggle in, fall down.

PIERCE. FIVE GODDAMN MILES!

All are in extreme pain.

KRESS. MOTHER-GODDAMN-BITCH—I NEVER RAN NO FIVE GODDAMN MILES IN MY LIFE. YOU GOTTA BE CRAZY TO RUN FIVE GODDAMN MILES. . . .

PARKER. I hurt. I hurt all over. I hurt, Kress. Oh, Christ.

PIERCE. There are guys spread from here to Range Two. You can be proud you made it, Parker. The whole company, man—they're gonna be comin' in for the next ten days.

And Parker yells in pain.

KRESS. Pierce, what's wrong with Parker?

PARKER. SHIT TOO, YOU MOTHER!

KRESS. It'll pass, Parker. Don't worry. Just stay easy.

(*While a little separate from the others, Pavlo is about to begin doing push-ups. He is very tired; it hurts him to do what he's doing.*)

Oh, Hummel, no. Hummel, please.

(*Pavlo is doing the push-ups, breathing the count, wheezing, gasping.*)

Hummel, you're crazy. You really are. He really is, Parker. Look at him. I hate crazy people. I hate 'em. YOU ARE REALLY CRAZY, HUMMEL. STOP IT OR I'LL KILL YOU. (*As Pavlo pivots into a sit-up position*) I mean, I wanna know how much money this platoon lost to that thief we got among us.

PIERCE. Three hundred and twelve dollars.

KRESS. What're you gonna do with all that money?

PAVLO. Spend it. Spend it.

KRESS. Something gonna be done to you! You hear me, Weird Face? You know what's wrong with you? You wouldn't know cunt if your nose was in it. You never had a piece a ass in your life.

There is a loud blast on a whistle.

PAVLO. Joanna Sorrentino ga' me so much ass my mother called her a slut.

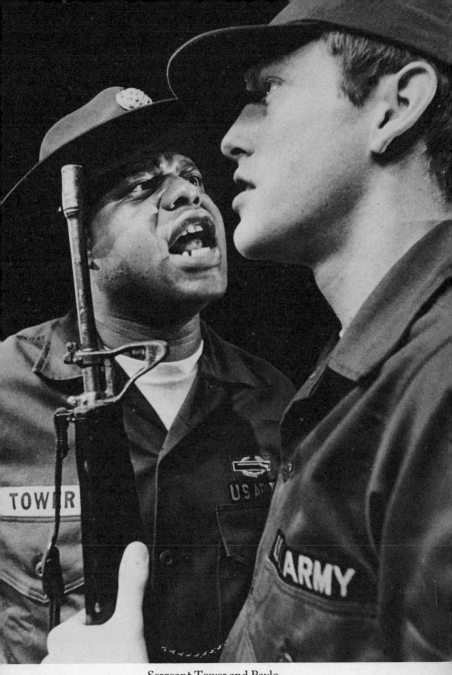

Sergeant Tower and Pavlo

KRESS. YOU FUCKING IDIOT!

Again the whistle.

PIERCE. Oh, Christ . . .

PAVLO. Let's go. LET'S GO. LET'S GET IT.

KRESS. Shut up.

PAVLO, *moving.* Let's GO, GO, GO—

All start to exit.

KRESS. SHUT YOUR MOUTH, ASSHOLE!

PAVLO. LET'S—GO, GO, GO, GO, GO, GO, GO . . . *(yelling, leading, yelling, as all ran off stage).*

Simultaneously, in the light on the opposite side of the stage, two soldiers—the corporal and Hendrix—are seen with pool cues at a pool table. There are no pool balls: the game will be pantomime; they use a cue ball to shoot and work with.

HENDRIX. You break.

CORPORAL. Naw, man, I shoot break on your say so, when I whip your ass, you'll come cryin'. You call.

He flips a coin, as Pavlo comes running back to get his helmet, which lies near where he was doing the push-ups.

HENDRIX. Heads.

CORPORAL. You got it.

Pavlo, scurrying off with his helmet, meets Sgt. Tower entering from opposite side.

SGT. TOWER. Trainee, go clean the dayroom. Sweep it up.

PAVLO. Pardon, Sergeant? I forgot my helmet . . .

SGT. TOWER. Go clean the dayroom, Trainee.

Pavlo runs off, as at the pool game Hendrix shoots break.

CORPORAL. My . . . my . . . my. . . . Yes sir. You're gonna be tough all right. That was a pretty damn break all right. *(Moving now to position himself for his shot.)* Except you missed all the holes. Didn't nobody tell you you were supposed to knock the little balls in the little holes?

PAVLO, *entering.* Sergeant Tower said for me to sweep up the day-room.

HENDRIX. And that's what you do—you don't smile, laugh, or talk; you sweep.

CORPORAL. You know what "buck a ball" means, Trainee?

PAVLO. What?

CORPORAL. Trainee's rich, Hendrix. Can't go to town, got money up the ass.

PAVLO. Sure I know what "buck a ball" means.

CORPORAL. Ohh, you hustlin' trainee motherfucker. New game. Right now. Rack 'em up!

Hendrix moves as if to rerack the balls.

PAVLO. You sayin' I can play?

CORPORAL. Hendrix, you keep an eye out for anybody who might not agree Trainee can relax a bit. You break, man.

PAVLO. I'll break.

CORPORAL. That's right.

PAVLO. You been to the war, huh? That's a First Division patch you got there, ain't it? (*Shooting first shot, missing, not too good.*)

CORPORAL. That's right.

PAVLO. Where at?

CORPORAL. How many wars we got?

PAVLO. I mean exactly where.

CORPORAL, *lining up his shot.* Di An. Ever hear of it?

PAVLO. Sure.

CORPORAL. Not much of a place but real close to Da Nang. (*He shoots, watches, moves for the next shot.*)

PAVLO. You up there too?

CORPORAL. Where's that?

PAVLO. By Da Nang.

(*The corporal is startled by Pavlo knowing this. He shoots and misses.*)

I mean, I thought Di An was more down by Saigon. D Zone. Down there. They call that D Zone, don't they?

CORPORAL. You're right, man; you know your shit. We got us a map-readin' motherfucker, Hendrix. Yeh, I was by Saigon, Hummel.

PAVLO. I thought so.

CORPORAL. Your shot.

He has moved off to the side where Hendrix has a hip flask of whiskey.

PAVLO, *moving for his shot.* Big Red One, man, I'd be proud wearin' that. (*He shoots and misses.*) Shit.

CORPORAL, *moving again to the table.* Good outfit. Top kinda outfit. Mean bastards, all of 'em. Every place we went, man we used ta tear 'em a new asshole, you can believe me. (*Shooting, making it, he moves on.*) I'm gonna win all your damn money, man. You got your orders yet for where you go when you're finished with basic?

PAVLO. No.

CORPORAL. Maybe if you're lucky, you'll get infantry, huh? Yeh, yeh, I seen some shit, you can believe me. (*And he moves about the table, shooting, shooting, as he speaks.*) But you go over there, that's what you're goin' for. To mess with them people, because they don't know nothin'. Them slopes; man they're the stupidest bunch a people anybody ever saw. It don't matter what you do to 'em or what you say, man they just look at you. They're some kinda goddamn phenomenon, man. Can of bug spray buy you all the ass you can handle in some places. Insect repellent, man. You ready for that? You give 'em can a bug spray, you can lay their fourteen-year-old daughter. Not that any of 'em screw worth a shit. (*He thinks it all interesting.*)

You hear a lot of people talkin' Airborne, One Seventy-third, Hundred and First, Marines, but you gotta go some to beat the First Division. I had a squad leader, Sergeant Tinden. He'd been there two goddamn years when I got there, so he knew the road, man; he knew his way. So we was comin' into this village once, the whole company, and it was supposed to be secure. We was Charlie Company and Alpha'd been through already, left a guard. And we was lead platoon and lead squad, and comin' toward us on the path is this old man, he musta been a hundred, about three foot tall, and he's got this little girl by the hand and she's maybe a half-step behind him. He's wavin' at us, "Okay, okay, GI." And she's wavin', too, but she ain't sayin' nothin', but there's this funny noise you can hear, a kind of cryin' like. *(He still moves about, shooting.)* Anyway, I'm next to the Sarge and he tells this old boy to stop, but they keep comin' like they don't understand, smilin' and wavin', so the Sarge says for 'em to stop in Vietnamese and then I can see that the kid is cryin'; she's got big tears runnin' outa her eyes, and her eyes are gettin' bigger and bigger and I can see she's tuggin' at the old man's hand to run away but he holds her and he hollers at her and I'm thinkin', "Damn, ain't that a bitch, she's so scared of us." And Tinden, right then, man he dropped to his knees and let go two bursts— first the old man, then the kid—cuttin' them both right across the face, man you could see the bullets walkin'. It was somethin'.

(He sets and takes his shot. He flops the cue onto the table.)

You owe me, man; thirteen bucks. But I'm superstitious, so we'll make it twelve.

(Pavlo pulls out a wad of money to pay.)

That's right. My ole daddy—the last day he saw me—he tole me good—"Don't you ever run on nobody, Boy, or if you do I hope there's somebody there got sense enough to shoot you down. Or if I hear you got away, I'll kill you myself." There's folks like that runnin' loose, Hummel. My ole man. You dig it.

(But Pavlo doesn't and he stares.)

What the fuck are you lookin' at?

PAVLO. I don't know why he shot . . . them.

CORPORAL. Satchel charges, man. The both of them, front and back. They had enough TNT on 'em to blow up this whole damn state and the kid got scared. They was wearing it under their clothes.

PAVLO. And he knew . . .

CORPORAL. That's right. Been around, so he knew. You ready, Hendrix?

They are moving to exit.

HENDRIX. Ain't that some shit, Hummel? Ain't that the way to be?

Parker can be seen far across the stage in dimness. Near him, Kress and three or four other soldiers crouch among the beds.

PARKER. Dear Mother. It was the oddest thing last night. I sat near my bunk, half awake, half asleep . . .

CORPORAL. You keep your ear to the ground, Hummel, you're gonna be all right. *(Exiting)* We'll see you around.

PAVLO. Just to see and to move; just to move.

He mimes with his broom the firing of a rifle, while Ardell stares and lunges suddenly backwards, rapidly hauling the table off.

PARKER, *loudly and flamboyantly.* Yes, yes, good Mother, I could not sleep, I don't know why. And then for further reasons that I do not know, I happened to look behind me and there . . . was a space ship, yes a space ship, green and golden, good Mother, come down to the sand of our Georgia home. A space ship . . .

(Pavlo wanders nearer. Parker glances toward Kress—who is kneeling with a blanket—and the others.)

And out of it, leaping they came, little green men no larger than pins. "Good Lord in Heaven," said I to myself, "what do they want? Sneaking among us, ever in silence, ever in stealth." Then I saw Hummel. "Hummel is coming," said I. "I will ask Hummel," said I to myself. "Hummel is coming."

(Pavlo enters.)

THIEF!

And the blanket is thrown over him. He is dragged to the floor. They beat and kick him. Call him "thief." He cries out. Squirms. A second blanket is thrown upon him, a mattress—it is his own

*bedding. As they beat and kick him, a whistle blows. All go run-
ning out, grabbing rifles and helmets, to form up for bayonet
practice where Sgt. Tower awaits them.*

*Pavlo emerges from beneath the blankets and no one is there
but Ardell.*

PAVLO. Didn't I do enough push-ups? How many do you have to
do, Ardell?

ARDELL. You got to understand, Pavlo, it fun sometimes to get a
man the way they got you. Come down on him, maybe pivot
kick. Break his fuckin' spine. Do him, man. Do . . . him . . .
good.

SGT. TOWER, *atop his platform, bayonet in hand.* You got to know
this bayonet shit, Gen'lmen, else you get recycled, you be back
to learn it all again. Eight more beautiful weeks in the armpit a
the nation. Else you don't get recycled, you get killed. Then you
wish for maybe half a second you been recycled. Do you know
the spirit of the bayonet is to kill? What is the spirit of the bayonet?

THE MEN. To kill!

*While Pavlo stirs about, Pierce enters the barracks. He is dishev-
eled, a little drunk.*

SGT. TOWER. You sound like pussies. You sound like slits.

THE MEN. TO KILL!

SGT. TOWER. You sound like pussies.

THE MEN. TO KILL!

*Pavlo, sensing Pierce, hurriedly opens his footlocker, digs out a
book, which he tries to pretend to read.*

PIERCE. Look at you. Ohhh, you know how much beer I hadda
drink to get fucked up on three-two beer? Hummel, look at me.
You think it's neat to be a squad leader? It's not neat to be a
squad leader.

(Pavlo reads from the little book.)

I hear you got beat up this afternoon.

PAVLO. I got a blanket party.

PIERCE. You're in my squad and other guys in my squad beat you, man; I feel like I oughta do somethin'. I'm older, see. Been to college a little; got a wife. And I'm here to tell you, even with all I seen, sometimes you are unbelievable, Hummel.

PAVLO. I don't care. I don't care.

PIERCE. I mean, I worry about you and the shit you do, man.

PAVLO. You do what you want, Pierce.

PIERCE. I mean, that's why people are after you, Hummel. That's why they fuck with you.

PAVLO. I'm trying to study my Code a Conduct, Pierce, you mind? It's just not too damn long to the proficiency test. Maybe you oughta be studyin' your Code a Conduct too, insteada sneakin' off to drink at the PX.

PIERCE. I wanna know how you got those rocks down your rifle. It's a two-mile walk out to the rifle range, and you got rocks in your barrel when we get there. That's what I'm talkin' about.

PAVLO. I don't know how that happened.

PIERCE. And every fight you get into, you do nothin' but dance, man. Round in a circle, bobbin' and weavin' and gettin' smacked in the mouth. Man, you oughta at least try and hit somebody. *(And then, suddenly, strangely, he is laughing.) Jesus Christ,* Hummel, what's wrong with you? We're in the shower and I tell you to maybe throw a punch once in a while, step with it, pivot, so you try it right there on that wet floor and damn near kill yourself smashin' into a wall.

PAVLO. Fuck you, Pierce.

PIERCE. Fuck you, Hummel.

Silence.

PAVLO. You know somethin', Pierce. My name ain't even really Pavlo Hummel. It's Michael Hummel. I had it legally changed. I had my name changed.

PIERCE. You're puttin' me on.

PAVLO. No, no, and someday, see, my father's gonna say to me,

"Michael, I'm so sorry I ran out on you," and I'm gonna say, "I'm not Michael, Asshole. I'm not Michael anymore." Pierce? You weren't with those guys who beat up on me, were you?

PIERCE. No.

Pavlo begins making his bunk.

ARDELL. Sometimes I look at you, I don't know what I think I'm seein', but it sooo simple. You black on the inside. In there where you live, you that awful hurtin' black so you can't see yourself no way. Not up or down or in or out.

SGT. TOWER—*down from the platform, he moves among the men.* There ain't no army in the world got a shorter bayonet than this one we got. Maneuverability. It the only virtue. You got to get inside that big long knife that other man got. What is the spirit of the bayonet?

THE MEN. TO KILL!

SGT. TOWER. You sound like pussies.

THE MEN. TO KILL!

SGT. TOWER. You sound like slits.

THE MEN. TO KILL!

SGT. TOWER. EN GARDE!

THE MEN. AGGGH!

SGT. TOWER. LONG THRUST, PARRY LEFT . . . WHO-OOOOO!

(And the men growl and move, one of them stumbling, falling down, clumsy, embarrassed.)

Where you think you are? You think you in the movies? This here real life, Gen'lmen. You actin' like there ain't never been a war in this world. Don't you know what I'm sayin'? You got to want to put this steel into a man. You got to want to cut him, hurt him, make him die. You got to want to feel the skin and muscle come apart with the push you give. It come to you in the wood. RECOVER AND HOLD!

THE MEN. AGGGH!

They yell and growl with each thrust. Another falls, gets up.

SGT. TOWER. EN GARDE!

THE MEN. AGGGH!

SGT. TOWER. Lookin' good, lookin' good. Only you ain't mean.

(The men growl.)

How come you ain't mean?

(The men growl.)

HORIZONTAL BUTT-STROKE SERIES, WHOOO!

(And they move, making the thrust, recovery, upper-cutting butt stroke, horizontal butt stroke, and downward slash. The growling and yelling get louder.)

Look at you; look at you. Ohhh, but you men put into my mind one German I saw in the war. I got one bullet left, don't think I want to shoot it, and here come this goddamned big-assed German. "Agggghhhh," I yell to him and it a challenge and he accept. "Agggghhhh," he say to me and set hisself and I just shoot him. Boom! Ohhh, he got a look on his face like I never saw before in my life. He one baffled motherfucker, Jim.

Without command, the men begin to march.

ARDELL, *singing*. ONCE A WEEK I GET TO TOWN . . .

THE MEN. THEY SEE ME COMIN', THEY ALL LAY DOWN.

ARDELL. IF I HAD A LOWER I.Q. . . .

All are marching, exiting.

THE MEN. I COULD BE A SERGEANT TOO.

SGT. TOWER. LORD HAVE MERCY, I'M SO BLUE. . . .

THE MEN. LORD HAVE MERCY, I'M SO BLUE. . . .

SGT. TOWER. IT SIX MORE WEEKS TILL I BE THROUGH. . . .

THE MEN. IT SIX MORE WEEKS TILL I BE THROUGH.

SGT. TOWER. SOUND OFF!

THE MEN. ONE—TWO.

Burns, Pierce, and another soldier enter the barracks area still singing, as others are exiting, and these three men set up a crap game on a footlocker.

SGT. TOWER. SOUND AGAIN!

THE MEN. THREE—FOUR.

Pavlo, Hinkle, and others enter.

SGT. TOWER. COUNT CADENCE, COUNT.

THE MEN. ONE, TWO, THREE, FOUR. ONE, TWO, THREE, FOUR. ONE, TWO, THREE, FOUR.

And they are all spread about the barracks, reading, sleeping.

PAVLO, *to Hinkle (as the crap game goes on nearby)*. Can you imagine that, Hinkle? Just knowin'. Seein' nothin' but bein' sure enough to gun down two people. They had TNT on 'em; they was stupid slopeheads. That Sergeant Tinden saved everybody's life. I get made anything but infantry, I'm gonna fight it, man. I'm gonna fight it. You wanna go infantry with me, Hinkle? You're infantry and good at it too, you're your own man, I'm gonna wear my uniform everywhere when I'm home, Hinkle. My mother's gonna be so excited when she sees me. She's just gonna yell. I get nervous when I think about if she should hug me. You gonna hug your mother when you get home?

HINKLE. My mom's a little bitty skinny woman.

PAVLO. I don't know if I should or shouldn't.

HINKLE. What's your mom like?

PIERCE. You tellin' him about your barn-house exploits, Hinkle?

HINKLE. Oh, no.

PIERCE. Hinkle says he screwed sheep. He tellin' you that, Hummel?

PARKER. How about pigs, Hinkle?

HINKLE. Oh, yeh.

KRESS. I'm tellin' you, Parker, it was too much; all that writin' and shit, and runnin' around. They ain't got no right to test you; proficiency test, proficiency test; I don't even know what a proficiency is—goddamn people—crawlin' and writin'—I'm tellin' you they ain't got no right to test you. They get you here, they mess with you—they let you go. Who says they gotta test you?

PIERCE, *who has the dice and is laying down money.* Who's back, man? I'm shootin' five.

KRESS. I got so nervous in hand-to-hand, I threw a guy against the wall. They flunked me for bein' too rough.

PIERCE. Who's back, man?

KRESS. I'll take three.

He puts down money, while Parker drops a couple of ones.

I get recycled, I'll kill myself, I swear it.

(As Pierce is shaking the dice, saying over and over, "Karen loves me, Karen loves me.")

I'll cut off my ear.

PIERCE, *throwing the dice.* Karen says I'm *good!*

KRESS. Goddamn! Shit! How they do it again, Parker?

PARKER. Pierce, you're incredible.

KRESS. Parker!

PARKER. They add up your scores, man; your PT, plus your rifle, plus the score they got today. Then they divide by three. *(Throwing down a five)* You lettin' it ride, Pierce?

PIERCE. Karen loves me.

KRESS, *putting in money.* Where they get the three?

PARKER. There's three events, man.

PIERCE, *throwing the dice.* Karen says, "I know the *road!*"

KRESS. You fucking asshole.

PARKER. Goddamnit, Pierce!

PIERCE. Who wants me? Back man's got no heart. Shootin' twenty I come seven or eleven—double or nothin'. Whose twenty says I can't come for all out of the gate? . . .

A soldier enters on the run.

SOLDIER. Tower's right behind me; he's got the scores.

General commotion as they hide the dice and the money, and Sgt. Tower strides across the stage and enters their area.

PIERCE. TENHUT!

All come to attention before their bunks.

SGT. TOWER. AT EASE!

(Men to parade rest.)

Gen'lmen. It's truth-and-consequences time. The sad tidings and *(handing a paper to Pierce for him to post)* the glad tidings. You got two men in this platoon didn't make it. They Burn and Kress. They gonna have to stay here eight more weeks, and if they as dumb as it look, maybe eight more after that and eight fuckin' more. The rest a you people, maybe you ain't got no spectacular qualities been endowed upon my mind, but you goin' home when you figured. *(He turns, leaving.)*

PIERCE. TENHUT!

SGT. TOWER. Carry on.

They are silent. Kress stands. All start talking and yelling at once.

PIERCE. Lemme holler . . . just one . . . time, lemme holler . . .

HINKLE. Mother, mother, make my bed!

A SOLDIER, *at the bulletin board.* Me! My name! Me!

PIERCE. AGGGGGGGGGHHHHHHHHHHHHHHHHHHHAAAA!

PARKER. Lemme just pack my bags!

HENDRIX, *entering with civilian clothes, shirt and trousers on a hanger, hat on his head.* Lookee—lookee—

HINKLE. What're them funny clothes?

PIERCE. CIVILIAN CLOTHES! CIVILIAN—

HINKLE. CI-WHO-LIAN?

PIERCE. PEOPLE OUTSIDE, MAN! THAT'S WHY THEY

AIN'T ALL FUNNY AND GREEN, BECAUSE YOU'RE OUTSIDE WHEN YOU WEAR 'EM. YOU'RE BACK ON THE BLOCK, BACK IN THE WORLD!

PAVLO, *standing on his bed.* DON'T NOBODY HEAR ME CALLIN' "KRESS!" *(He has said the name during the yelling.)* I think we oughta tell him how sorry we are he didn't make it. I'm gonna. I'm gonna tell him. I'm sorry Kress, that you're gonna be recycled and you're not goin' home. I think we're all sorry. I bet it's kinda like gettin' your head caught in a blanket, the way you feel. It's a bad feelin', I bet, and I think I understand it even if I am goin' back where there's lights and it's pretty. I feel sorry for you, Kress, I just wanna laugh, I feel so sorry—

(And Kress, leaping, pushes him. Pavlo staggers backward.)

Sonofabitch, what're you—SONOFABITCH!

He swings a wild right hand. They flail and crash about. Kress grabs Pavlo's wrist, drawing him forward into a hammer lock.

KRESS. Down. *(Then lifting)* Don't you hear me? Down, I'm sayin'. Don't you hear me? Thata boy. . . . Called crawlin'. . . .

(And Pavlo is thrown to the floor, Kress on top of him.)

You got the hang of it . . . now. . . . Crawlin'. . . . Yeh. Now I'm gonna ask you something? Okay?

PAVLO. . . . okay . . .

KRESS. What I'd like to know is who is it in this platoon steals money from his buddies? Who is it don't know how to talk decent to nobody? and don't have one goddamn friend? Who is that person? You tell me, Hummel? The name a that person passed his test today by cheatin'.

PAVLO. I don't . . . know . . .

KRESS, *working the arm.* Who?

PAVLO. No—

(And the arm is twisted again.)

Stop him, somebody. Pierce. You're my squad leader, Pierce. Ohhhh . . . Pierce, please . . . Aggghhhh . . . Pierce . . .

KRESS. WHO?

And Pavlo yells.

PIERCE. Ease off a little. . . .

KRESS. I CAN'T HEAR YOU!

PIERCE. Kress, I—

PAVLO. HUMMEL!

KRESS. WHAT? WHAT?

PAVLO. HUMMEL! HUMMEL!

KRESS. WHAT?

PAVLO. HUMMEL! HUMMEL! He did 'em. All of those things. All of 'em. He cheated. He cheated. HUMMEL! HUM—

PIERCE. Kress, goddamnit. GODDAMNIT! *(Leaping, he lifts Kress away from Pavlo and throws him sideways.)*

KRESS. What? What you want, Corporal? Don't mess with me, man. *(Staring at Pierce, who is between him and Pavlo, Kress backs away, yet he rages.)* Don't mess with Kress. Not when he's feelin' bad. He'll kill ya, honest to God. He'll pee in your dead mouth.

And Pavlo rushes at Kress, howling.

PIERCE. Noooooooooo. *(Seizes Pavlo, pushing him back.)*

PAVLO *(as Kress storms out and the other soldiers follow in an effort to console him).* I'm all right. I'm all right. I do all right!

PIERCE. Will you listen to me, man; you're goin' home; not Kress. You got him.

PAVLO. Fucking asshole!

PIERCE. Will you listen? *(Shoving Pavlo, scolding him)* You gotta learn to think, Hummel. You gotta start puttin' two and two together so they fit. You beat him; you had ole Kress beat and then you fixed it so you hadda lose. You went after him so he hadda be able to put you down.

PAVLO. I just wanted to let him know what I thought.

PIERCE. No, no!

Parker, Kress, Pierce, and Pavlo

PAVLO. He had no call to hit me like that. I was just talkin'—

PIERCE. You dared him, man.

PAVLO. You shoulda stopped him, that's the problem. You're the squad leader. That's just this whole damn army messin' with me and it ain't ever gonna end but in shit. How come you're a squad leader? Who the fuck are you? I'm not gonna get a chance at what I want. Not ever. Nothin' but shit. They're gonna mess with me—make a clerk outta me or a medic or truck driver, a goddamn moron—or a medic—a nurse—a fuckin' Wac with no tits—or a clerk, some little goddamn twerp of a guy with glasses and no guts at all. So don't gimme shit about what I done, Pierce, it's what you done and done and didn't—

(During this whole thing, Pierce has moved about straightening the bunks and footlockers, and Pavlo, in growing desperation, has followed him. Now Pierce, in disgust, starts to leave.)

That's right; keep on walkin' away from your duties, keep—

PIERCE. You're happy as a pig in shit, I don't know why I keep thinkin' you ain't.

PAVLO. I am not.

PIERCE. Up to your eyeballs!

PAVLO. I'm gonna kill myself, Pierce! *(It bursts out of him.)*

PIERCE. If you weren't in my squad, I'd spit in your face. . . .

He pivots and goes off after Kress and the other soldiers.

PAVLO, *rocking backward, then bowing forward.* Fuck you, fuck you.

(He is alone and yelling after them as Ardell enters.)

I hate you goddamn people!

ARDELL. I know.

PAVLO. Ardell.

At his footlocker, Pavlo rummages.

ARDELL. I know. I know. All you life like a river and there's no water all around—this emptiness—you gotta fill it. Gotta get water. You dive, man, you dive off a stone wall

(Pavlo has a canteen and paper bag in his hands.)

into the Hudson River waitin' down dark under you. For a second, it's all air . . . so free. . . . Do you know the distance you got to fall? You think you goin' up. Don't nobody fall up, man. Nobody.

PAVLO. What is it? I want to know what it is. The thing that sergeant saw to make him know to shoot that kid and old man. I want to have it, know it, be it.

ARDELL. I know.

PAVLO. When?

ARDELL. Soon.

PAVLO. If I could be bone, Ardell; if I could be bone. In my deepest part or center, if I could be bone.

Taking a bottle from the bag, he takes pills, washes them down with water, and crawls under the covers of his bunk, while Sgt. Tower, already on the platform, speaks.

SGT. TOWER. Now I'm gonna tell you gen'lmen how you find you way when you lost. You better listen up. What you do, you find the North Star and the North Star show you true north accurate all year round. You look for the Big Dipper and there are two stars at the end a that place in the stars that look like the bowl on the dipper and they called the pointer. They them two stars at where the water would come out the dipper if it had some water and out from them on a straight line you gonna see this big damn star and that the North Star and it show you north and once you know that, Gen'lmen, you can figure the rest. You ain't lost no more.

THE MEN, *beginning to enter to position themselves for the next scene.* YESSSS, SERGEANT!

SGT. TOWER. I hope so. I do hope so. . . .

Pierce, Parker, and others set up a card game on a footlocker.

KRESS, *passing the bunk where Pavlo is a lump beneath his blanket.* I wonder what the fuckin', chimney-shittin' shit is doin' now?

Hinkle settles curiously on the bunk next to Pavlo.

PARKER. You gonna see me Pierce?

PIERCE. And raise you.

PARKER. Ten ta one, he's under there jerkin' off!

HINKLE, *bending near to Pavlo.* No, no, he's got this paper bag and everything smells funny. Y'all some kind of acrobat, Hummel?

KRESS. He's got some chick's bicycle seat in a bag, man.

HINKLE. And the noises he's makin'.

PIERCE. Poor pathetic motherfucker.

KRESS. He ain't pathetic.

PIERCE. He is too.

PARKER. Under there pounding his pud.

KRESS. You musta not seen many pathetic people, you think he's pathetic.

PIERCE. I seen plenty.

PARKER. Call.

PIERCE, *laying down his cards.* Full boat. Jacks and threes!

PARKER. Jesus Goddamn Christ.

HINKLE. I was wonderin' can ah look in you all's bag, Hummel? *(He reaches under the blanket.)*

PARKER. Jesus Goddamn Christ.

HINKLE. Ohhhh . . . it's . . . you been sniffin' airplane glue. . . . *(And he laughs, turns toward the others.)* Hummel's been sniffin' airplane glue.

KRESS. ATTAWAY TO GO, HUMMEL.

HINKLE, *holding the bottle.* An' where's all the asp'rins . . . ?

PAVLO. Tumtum Pavlo.

HINKLE. You all kiddin' me.

PAVLO. No.

HINKLE. Y'all ate 'em?

PAVLO. Yeah!

HINKLE. Hey y'all. . . . *(To Pavlo)* Was it full?

Pavlo attempts to sit up, flops back down.

PAVLO. Tippy top.

HINKLE. Hummel just ate—*(examining the bottle)* one hundred asp'rins. Hummel just ate 'em.

KRESS. Attaway to go, Hummel.

PARKER. Nighty-night.

HINKLE. Won't it hurt him, Pierce?

KRESS. Kill him probably.

PARKER. Hopefully.

KRESS. Hinkle, ask him did he use chocolate syrup?

HINKLE. He's breathin' kinda funny, Pierce, don't you think?

KRESS. Hummel does everything funny.

PIERCE, *beginning to deal.* Five cards, Gen'lmen; jacks or better.

HINKLE. Pierce.

PIERCE. Hummel, you stop worryin' that boy. Tell him no headache big enough in the world, you're gonna take a hundred asp'rins.

(Slight pause. Kress begins imitating Pavlo's odd breathing.)

How come everybody's all the time bustin' up my good luck.

BURNS. Shit, man, he took a hundred asp'rins, he wouldn't be breathin' period.

RYAN. Sounds like a goddamn tire pump.

BURNS. Hummel, TENHUT!

PIERCE. Hummel, you just jivin' cause you don't know what else to do, or did you eat them pills?

BURNS. Tryin' to blow himself up like a balloon . . . drift away. Float outa the fort.

Parker begins to imitate Kress imitating Pavlo's breathing.

RYAN. He's fakin', man.

BURNS. How you know?

RYAN. They'd kill you like a bullet.

HINKLE. Get over here, Pierce!

KRESS. How come the army don't thow him out, Parker?

PARKER. Army likes weird people, Kress.

KRESS. I hate weird people.

PARKER. Sure you do.

KRESS. Weird chimney-shittin', friendless, gutless, cheatin' . . .

Pierce is examining Pavlo. Pavlo makes a sound and then begins to cough.

PIERCE. NOOO! NOT IN MY SQUAD, YOU MOTHER. GET UP!

(He is trying to get Pavlo to his feet; another soldier is helping.)

YOU SILLY SONOFABITCH. We got to walk him.

(Pavlo is feebly resisting.)

Hinkle, doubletime it over the orderly room.

HINKLE. Right.

PIERCE. Tell 'em we got a guy over here took a hundred asp'rins, they should get an ambulance.

HINKLE, *turning to head for the door.* Right.

KRESS. Hinkle!

HINKLE, *hesitating.* Yeh!

KRESS. Pick me up a Coke on your way back.

PIERCE. Hold him steady. I think we oughta get him outside, more air.

ARDELL, *standing over near the base of the tower.* Pavlo. You gonna have ambulances and sirens and all kinds a good shit. Ain't you somethin'? It gonna be a celebration. C'mon over here.

(As if Ardell's voice draws them, Pierce and the other soldier lug

Pavlo toward the tower: they lay him down, remove all clothes from him but his underwear and T-shirt.)

Pavlo! Look at you. You got people runnin' around like a bunch a fools. That what you wanted? Yeah, that what you want! They sayin' "Move him. Lift him. Take his shirt off." They walkin' you around in the air. They all thinkin' about you, anyway. But what you doin' but cryin'? You always think you signifyin' on everybody else, but all you doin' is showin' your own fool self. You don't know nothin' about showboatin', Pavlo. You hear me? Now you get on up off that floor. You don't get up, man, I blow a motherfuckin' whistle up side you head. I blow it loud. YOU THINK YOU GOT A MOTHERFUCKIN' WHISTLE IN YOUR BRAIN.

(Pierce and the other man have turned away. Everything Pavlo does is performed in the manner of a person alone: as if Ardell is a voice in his head. The light perhaps suggests this. Kress, all others, are frozen.)

I'm tellin' you how to be. That right.

(Pavlo slumps back down.)

Ohhh, don't act so bad; you actin', man. What you expect, you go out get you head smokin' on all kinds a shit sniffin' that goddamn glue, then fallin' down all over yourself. Man, you lucky you alive, carryin' on like that.

(Pavlo is doubled over.)

Ain't doin' you no good you wish you dead, 'cause you ain't, man. Get on up.

(Pavlo takes a deep breath and stands.)

You go in the latrine now, get you a bromo, you wash off you face . . .

(Pavlo exits, staggering.)

Then get you ass right back out here. And you don't need no shave, man, you ain't got no beard no ways. *(Sees Pavlo's uniform lying on the floor.)* What kinda shit this? Your poor ole Sarge see this, he sit down on the ground and he cry, man. Poor ole Sarge, he work himself like he crazy tryin' ta teach you so you can act like a man. An' what you do? *(Turning suddenly, yelling after Pavlo) Pavlo!* You diddlin' in there, you take this long. And you bring out you other uniform. We gonna shape you up.

(Pavlo enters carrying military dress uniform in a clothing bag, which he hangs on the tower.)

It daytime, man, you goin' out struttin'. You goin' out standin' tall. You tear it open. Trousers first, man. Dig 'em out.

(Pavlo, having selected the trousers, moves as if to put them on.)

NOOOO! Damnit, ain't you got no sense at all?

(He has rushed to Pavlo, lifted the trouser bottoms off the floor.)

You drag 'em all over the floor like that, man, they gonna look like shit. Get up on this footlocker!

(Now Pierce and the other soldier move in to help Pavlo dress. All is ease now.)

That right, that it. Make 'em look like they got no notion at all what it like ta be dirty. Be clean, man. Yeh. Now the shirt.

(It is a ritual now: Pavlo must exert no effort whatsoever as he is transformed.)

Lemme look you brass over. Ain't too bad. It do. Lemme just touch 'em up a little. *(He brushes with his handkerchief at the brass.)* You put on you tie. Make you a big knot. Big knot make you look tall. Where you boots?

(And, finished with the jacket, Pierce and the other soldier move to the boots.)

Where you boots? An' you got some shades? Lemme get you some shades. *(Walking backward)* And tuck that tie square. Give her little loop she come off you throat high and pretty.

(As Ardell exits, Pavlo sits on the footlocker. Pierce and the other soldier kneel to put the boots onto him.)

HUT . . . HOO . . . HEE . . . HAW. . . . *(Singing)* IF I HAD A LOWER I.Q.

ALL THE MEN. IF I HAD A LOWER I.Q.

ARDELL. I COULD BE A SERGEANT TOO.

THE MEN. I COULD BE A SERGEANT TOO!

Across the back of the stage, two men march.

ARDELL. LORD HAVE MERCY, I'M SO BLUE.

The two men do an intricate drill-team step.

THE MEN. IT FOUR MORE WEEKS TILL I BE THROUGH.

The two men spin their rifles and strike the ground smartly with the butts, as Ardell returns, carrying a pair of sunglasses.

ARDELL. You gonna be over, man, I finish with you.

(Pavlo stands up fully dressed.)

You gonna be the fat rat, man; you eatin' cheese.

(Ardell moves about Pavlo, examining him, guiding him toward the tower. As Ardell talks, Pavlo climbs the tower and stands on it; Ardell joins him.)

OVER, BABY! Ardell can make you straight; you startin' ta look good now; you finish up, you gonna be the fattest rat, man, eatin' the finest cheese. Put you in good company, you wear that uniform. You go out walkin' on the street, people know you, they say, "Who that?" Somebody else say, "Man, he straight. He look good." Somebody else say, "That boy got pride." Yeh, baby, Pavlo, you gonna be over, man. You gonna be that fat fat rat, eatin' cheese, down on his knees, yeh, baby, doffin' his red cap, sayin', "Yes, Massa." You lookee out there.

(Both are atop the tower. Ardell is a little behind Pavlo and gesturing outward. Pavlo stands. He has sunglasses on.)

Who you see in that mirror, man? Who you see? That ain't no Pavlo Hummel. Noooo, man. That somebody else. An' he somethin' else.

(Pavlo is looking.)

Ohhh, you goin' out on the street, they gonna see you. Ardell tellin' you and Ardell know. You back on the block an' you goin' out struttin'. An' they gonna cry when they see you. You so pretty, baby, you gonna make 'em cry. You tell me you name, you pretty baby!

PAVLO, *snapping to attention.* PAVLO MOTHERHUMPIN' HUMMEL!

Blackout.

ACT TWO

Set changes: The debris of the bar wall remains upstage and stage right, though the barrel and crate are gone. Downstage and stage right there is a larger, more detailed version of the bar: metal wall, barrel used as table, two crates used as chairs, a footlocker off to the side, beer cans and bottles scattered about. The drill sergeant's tower remains. Far downstage and just a little left of center, a telephone sits on the floor near another footlocker. Stage left of the tower there is an army cot with a green but nonmilitary bedspread.

The lights come up on the men in formation. Pavlo is still atop the tower, standing, looking out as he was. The men face upstage. Standing at the rear of the set are the captain and Sgt. Tower. They face the men. Downstage stands Mickey, Pavlo's half-brother. Mickey wears slacks, T-shirt, shoes. He is standing as if looking into a mirror about to comb his hair; however he does not move. The captain, stiffly formal, addresses the troops.

CAPTAIN. As we enter now the final weeks of your basic training, I feel a certain obligation as your company commander to speak to you of the final purpose of what we have done here. Normally this is more difficult to make clear. Pleiku, Vietnam, is the purpose of what we have done here. A few nights ago, mortar and machine-gun fire in a sneak attack in the highlands killed nine Americans and wounded a hundred and forty serving at our camp there in Pleiku. In retaliation, a bombing of the North has begun, and it will continue until the government of Hanoi, battered and reeling, goes back to the North.

SGT. TOWER. Company, fall out!

And the troops scatter. Music starts from Mickey's radio. Pavlo descends, picks up duffle bag and AWOL bag. Mickey starts combing his hair.

PAVLO. Hey Mickey, it's me. I'm home! It's me. I'm home, I'm home.

MICKEY. Pavlo. Whata you say, huh? Hey, hey, what happened? You took so long. You took a wrong turn, huh? Missed your stop and now you come home all dressed up like a conductor. What happened? You were down in that subway so long they put you to work? Huh? Man, you look good though; you look good. Where were you again?

PAVLO. Georgia.

MICKEY. Hot as a bitch, right?

PAVLO. No. Cold.

MICKEY. In Georgia?

PAVLO. Yeh, it was real cold; we used to hide out in the furnace room every damn chance we ever got.

MICKEY. Hey, you want a drink? Damn that don't make much sense, does it?

PAVLO. What?

MICKEY. They send you to Georgia for the winter and it's like a witch's tit. Can you imagine that? A witch's tit? Eeeeeegggggg. Puts ice on your tongue. That ever happened to me, man, I'd turn in my tool. Ain't you gonna ask about the ole lady? How's she doin' and all that, cause she's doin' fine. Pickin' and plantin' daisies. Doin' fine.

(And Pavlo laughs, shaking his head, taking the drink Mickey has made him.)

Whatsa matter? You don't believe yo-yos can be happy? Psychotics have fun, man. You oughta know that.

PAVLO. I just bet she's climbin' some kinda wall. Some kinda wall and she's pregnant again, she thinks, or you are or me or somebody.

MICKEY. Noo, man, noo, it's everybody else now. Only nonfamily.

PAVLO, *laughing, loudly.* THAT'S ME AND YOU! NONFAM-ILY MOTHERFUCKERS!

MICKEY. All the dogs and women of the world!

PAVLO. Yeh, yeh, all the guys in the barracks used to think I was a little weird, so I'd—

MICKEY. You *are* a little weird—

PAVLO. Yeh, yeh, I'd tell 'em, "You think I'm weird, you oughta see my brother, Mickey. He don't give a big rat's ass for nothin' or nobody."

MICKEY. And did you tell 'em about his brains, too. And his wit and charm. The way his dick hangs to his knees—about his eighteen thou a year? Did you tell 'em all that sweet shit?

PAVLO. They said they hoped you died of all you got.

Mickey has been dressing as they speak, and now he wears a shirt and tie and suit coat.

MICKEY. How come the troops were thinkin' you weird? You doin' that weird stuff again. You say "Georgia" and "the army." For all I know you been downtown in the movies for the last three months and you bought that goddamn uniform at some junk shop.

PAVLO. I am in the army.

MICKEY. How do I know?

PAVLO. I'm tellin' you.

MICKEY. But you're a fuckin' liar; you're a fuckin' myth-maker.

PAVLO. I gotta go to Vietnam, Mickey.

MICKEY. Vietnam don't even exist.

PAVLO. I gotta go to it.

MICKEY. Arizona, man; that's where you're goin'. Wyoming.

PAVLO. Look at me! I'm different! I'm different than I was! *(This is with fury.)* I'm not the same anymore. I was an asshole. I'm not an asshole anymore. I'm not an asshole anymore! *(Silence as he*

Mickey and Pavlo

stares in anguish.) I came here to forgive you. I don't need you anymore.

MICKEY. You're a goddamn cartoon, you know that.

PAVLO, *rapidly, in a rush of words.* I'm happier now than I ever was, I got people who respect me. Lots of 'em. There was this guy Kress in my outfit. We didn't hit it off . . . and he called me out . . . he was gonna kill me, he said. Everybody tried to stop me because this guy had hurt a lot of people already and he had this uncle who'd taught him all about fightin' and this uncle has been executed in San Quentin for killing people. We went out back of the barracks. It went on and on, hitting and kicking. It went on and on; all around the barracks. The crowd right with us. And then . . . all of a sudden . . . this look came into his eye . . . and he just stopped . . . and reached down to me and hugged me. He just hugged and hugged me. And that look was in all their eyes. All the soldiers. I don't need you anymore, Mickey. I got real brothers now.

MICKEY. You know . . . if my father hadn't died, you wouldn't even exist.

PAVLO. No big thing! We got the same mother; that's shit enough. I'm gonna shower and shave, okay? Then we can go out drinkin'.

MICKEY. All those one-night stands. You ever think of that? Ghostly pricks. I used to hear 'em humpin' the ole whore. I probably had my ear against the wall the night they got you goin'.

PAVLO, *after a slight silence.* You seen Joanna lately?

MICKEY. Joanna?

PAVLO. Joanna. My ole girl. I thought maybe she probably killed herself and it was in the papers. You know, on account of my absence. But she probably did it in secret.

MICKEY. No doubt.

PAVLO. No doubt.

MICKEY. Ain't she the one who got married? I think the ole lady tole me Joanna got married and she was gonna write you a big letter all about it. Sure she was. Anyway, since we're speaking of old girls and pregnant people, I've got to go to this little party tonight. Got a good new sweet young thing and she thinks I'm better than her daddy. I've had a run of chicks lately you wouldn't believe, Pavlo. They give away ass like Red Cross girls dealin' out doughnuts. I don't understand how I get half a what I get. Oh, yeh, old lady comes and goes around here. She's the same old witch.

PAVLO. I'm gonna go see Joanna. I'll call her up. Use the magic fuckin' phone to call her up.

MICKEY. I'll give you call later on.

PAVLO. I'll be out, man. I'll be out on the street.

MICKEY, *exiting.* You make yourself at home.

And soldiers appear far upstage, marching forward, as Ardell, off to the side, counts cadence, and other soldiers appear at various points about the stage.

ARDELL. HUT . . . HOO . . . HEE . . .

SGT. TOWER, *entering as Pavlo, glancing at him, exits.* SAW SOME STOCKIN'S ON THE STREET . . .

THE MEN. WISHED I WAS BETWEEN THOSE FEET.

SGT. TOWER. WISHED I WAS BETWEEN THOSE FEET. HONEY, HONEY, DON'T YOU FROWN.

THE MEN. I LOVE YOU DRUNK AND LAYIN' DOWN.

SGT. TOWER. STANDIN' TALL AND LOOKIN' GOOD. WE BELONG IN HOLLYWOOD.

He is atop the tower, as the men come to a stomping halt.

THE MEN. WE BELONG IN HOLLYWOOD.

SGT. TOWER. Take five, Gen'lmen, but the smokin' lamp is not lit.

Pavlo is there, off to the side, disheveled, carrying a pint whiskey bottle. He undresses, speaking his anger, throwing his uniform down. The men are relaxing a little.

PAVLO. Stupid fuckin' uniform. Miserable hunk a green shit. Don't we go to good bars—why don't you work for me? And there's this really neat girl there sayin' to me how do I like bein' a robot? How do I like bein' one in a hundred million robots all marchin' in a row? Don't anybody understand about uniforms? I ain't no robot. You gotta have braid . . . ribbons and patches all about what you did. I got nothin'. What's so complicated? I look like nothin' cause I done nothin'. *(In his T-shirt and underwear, he kneels now with the bottle.)*

SGT. TOWER. Gen'lmen, you best listen up real close now, even though you restin'. Gonna tell you little bit about what you do you comin' through the woods, you find a man wounded in his chest. You gotta seal it off. That wound workin' like a valve, pullin' in air, makin' pressure to collapse that man's lung; you get him to breathe out and hold his breath. You apply the metal-foil side a the waterproof wrapping of the first-aid dressing, tie it off. Gonna hafta tie it extra; you use your poncho, his poncho, you get strips of cloth. You tear up you own damn shirt. I don't care. You let that boy have his lung. You let him breathe. AM I UN-DERSTOOD?

THE MEN. YES, SERGEANT!

SGT. TOWER. FALL IN!

(The men leap to attention.)

DISMISSED!

(And the troops run off, leaving Pavlo alone, in his underwear, near the bed.)

PAVLO. I wanna get laid . . . Bed . . . Bottle. *(Pause.)* I wanna get laid! I wanna get laid, Phone! You goddamn stuck-up motherin' phone. Need a piece of ass, Bed. Lemme walk on over to that phone. Lemme crawl on over to that phone. Lemme get there. Gonna outflank you. Goddamn army ant. Thas right. Thas right. Hello. *(He has crawled drunkenly to the phone and is dialing now.)* This is Pavlo, Joanna. Hello. Certainly of course. I'd be glad to screw your thingy with my thingy. BSZZZZZZZ . . .

WOMAN'S VOICE *(over the phone).* Hello?

PAVLO. BSZZZZZZZZZZZZZZZZZZZZZZZZZZZ . . .

WOMAN'S VOICE. Hello?

PAVLO. Little bitty creature . . . hello, hello. . . .

WOMAN'S VOICE. Who is this?

PAVLO. Hollering . . . hollering . . . poor creature . . . locked inside, can't get out, can't—

WOMAN'S VOICE. Pavlo?

PAVLO. Do you know me? Yes. Yes, it is me, Pavlo. Pavlo Hummel. . . . Joanna. . . . And I am calling to ask how can you have lived to this day away from me?

WOMAN'S VOICE. Pavlo, listen.

PAVLO. Yes. I am. I do.

WOMAN'S VOICE. This isn't Joanna.

PAVLO. What?

WOMAN'S VOICE. This is Mrs. Sorrentino, Pavlo. Joanna isn't here.

PAVLO. What?

WOMAN'S VOICE. I said "Joanna isn't here," Pavlo. This is her mother; may I have her call you?

PAVLO. What?

WOMAN'S VOICE. I said, "May I have her call you?" Or did you just call to say hello?

PAVLO. Who is this?

WOMAN'S VOICE. Pavlo, what's wrong with you?

PAVLO. Who are you? I don't know who this is. You get off the line, goddamnit, you hear me, or I'll report you to the telephone company. I'll report you to Bell Telephone. And G.E., too. And the Coke Company and General Motors.

(*The woman hangs up the phone.*)

You'll be hurtin' baby. I report you to all those people. Now you tell me where she is. Where is she?

And behind him a light pops on, a table lamp. His mother, a small, dark-haired woman, plump, fashionably dressed, has been there for some time, sitting in the dark, listening. She begins to speak almost at the same instant the light goes on.

MRS. HUMMEL. In Stratford, Connecticut, Pavlo. Pregnant more than likely. Vomiting in the morning. Yes . . . trying to . . . get . . . rid of . . . it. . . . Hello, Pavlo . . . I wrote you that. . . . I wrote you.

(Silence.)

Hello . . . Pavlo. I wrote you she was married. Why are you calling? Why?

(Silence.)

Pavlo? Listen, are you finished on the phone and could we talk a minute? I don't want to interrupt. . . . I only have a few . . . few things to say. They won't take long. I've been working since you've been gone. Did you know?

(As she continues to talk, Pavlo slowly hangs up the telephone and places it on the footlocker.)

Doing quite well. Quite well indeed. In a department store. Yes. One of the smaller ones. Yes. And we had an awful, awful shock there the other day and that's what I want to tell you about. There's a woman, Sally Kelly, and Ken was her son, in the army like you now, and he went overseas last August. Well, I talked to Sally when I went in at noon and she was in the lunchroom writing a little card to Ken and she let me read it. She knew that you were in the army so she said she was sure I knew the way it was consolation to write a little note. Then about five forty-five, I was working on the shoes and I saw two army officers come up the escalator and talk to one of the other clerks. I never gave them another thought and at six o'clock Sally came through and went down the escalator and made a remark to me and laughed a little and went on down. In about fifteen more minutes, I was waiting on a lady and she said to me, "Isn't that terrible about the lady's son who works downstairs?" I said, "Who?" She said, "The lady who works at your candy department just got word her son was killed in Vietnam." Well, I was really shook when I heard that and I said, "Oh, you must be mistaken. She just went downstairs from her supper hour and I talked to her and she was fine." She said, "Well, that's what I heard on the main floor." Well, I went right to the phone and called the reception desk and they said it was true. This is what happened, this is what I want to tell you. The officers had gone to Sally's house but no one was home so they talked to the neighbors and found out Sally worked at the store. So they went up to our receptionist and asked for our manager. He wasn't in so they asked for one of the men and Tommy Bottle came and they told him they needed his help because they had to tell one of the employees that her son was killed in Vietnam. Tommy really got shook, as you can imagine, and he took the officers to Mr. Brenner's office and closed the door. While they were in there, Sally came out of the lunchroom and came downstairs. Joyce, the girl who is the receptionist, knew by this time and Sally laughed when she went by and said that she better get to work or something like that. Joyce said later on that she could hardly look at her. Anyway, Tommy called the floorman from first floor to come up and he told him what had happened and then he had to go back down to first floor and tell Sally she was wanted in Mr. Brenner's office. She said, "Oh boy, what have I done now?" By the time she got to the fourth floor, the office door was open and she saw the two army men and said, "Oh, dear God, not Kenny." (*Pause.*) A mother . . . and her children should be as a tree and her branches. . . . A mother spends . . . but she gets . . . change. You think me a fool . . . don't you. There are many who do. (*Pause.*) He joined to be a mechanic and they transferred him to Infantry so he was killed on December first. So you see . . . I know what to expect. I know . . . what you're trying to do.

PAVLO. Who . . . was . . . my father? Where is he?

MRS. HUMMEL. You know that.

PAVLO. No, I want you to tell me.

MRS. HUMMEL. I've already told you.

PAVLO. No, where is he now? What did he look like?

MRS. HUMMEL. I wrote it all in a letter. I put it all in an envelope, I sealed it, mailed it.

PAVLO. I never got it.

MRS. HUMMEL. I think you did.

PAVLO. No!

MRS. HUMMEL. No, you had many fathers, many men, movie men, filmdom's great—all of them, those grand old men of yesteryear, they were your father. The Fighting Seventy-sixth, do you remember, oh, I remember, little Jimmy, what a tough little mite he was, and how he leaped upon that grenade, did you see, my God what a glory, what a glorious thing with his little tin hat.

PAVLO. My real father!

MRS. HUMMEL. He was like them, the ones I showed you in movies, I pointed them out.

PAVLO. What was his name?

MRS. HUMMEL. I've told you.

PAVLO. No. What was his name? I don't know what it was.

MRS. HUMMEL. Is it my fault you've forgotten?

PAVLO. You never told me.

MRS. HUMMEL. I did. I whispered it in your ear. You were three. I whispered the whole thing in your ear!

PAVLO. Lunatic!

MRS. HUMMEL. Nooooo!

PAVLO. Insane, hideous person!

MRS. HUMMEL. I've got to go to bed now. I have to get my rest.

(Her back is turned. She is walking to leave him.)

PAVLO, *yelling.* I picked this girl up in this bar tonight and when I took her home and got her to the door and kissed her, her tongue went into my mouth. I thought that meant she was going to let me into her apartment. "Don't get hurt," she said, "and get in touch when you get back; I'd love to see you." She knew I was going overseas; did you? And then the door was shut and all I wanted to say was, "What are you doing sticking your tongue in my mouth and then leaving me, you goddamn stuck-up motherin' bitch." But I didn't say anything.

MRS. HUMMEL, *as she leaves.* Yes . . . well . . . I'll . . . see you in the morning.

ARDELL, *who has been watching.* Oh, man, how come? You wanted to get laid, how come you didn't do like the ole Sarge told you steada gettin' all tore up with them walkin' blues? Take you a little money, the ole Sarge say, roll it up longways, put it in your fly, man, so it stickin' out. Then go on walkin' up and down the street, that green stickin' right outa your fly. You get laid. You got that money stickin' outa your fly, you get laid. You get your nut! How come you didn't do that?

OFFICER, *who has been standing on the rear platform at parade rest.* And the following will depart CONUS twelve August nineteen sixty-six for the Republic of Vietnam on assignment to the Twenty-third Field Hospital. Thomas. Simpson. Horner. Hinkle. Hummel.

PAVLO. I don't wanna be no medic!

And the bar music starts. Yen and Mamasan, an older Vietnamese woman, enter from one side of the stage. Sgt. Brisbey is calling from the other, and then his hospital bed on wheels is pushed on by two soldiers. Meanwhile Ardell has hauled off the footlocker with the telephone. Now visible on the floor is a pile of clothes, Pavlo's jungle fatigues, which he immediately starts getting into. Yen is at the bar. All this happens nearly simultaneously. Mamasan, scurrying about, exits.

YEN. Hey, GI cheap Charlie, you want one more beer?

JONES, *offstage.* One Bomniba, one beer.

SGT. BRISBEY. Pavlo.

YEN *(as Jones, in a bright-colored walking suit, enters).* EEEEEEaaaaaa? What you talk? One Bomniba, one beer. Same-same, huh? I no stand. What you want?

JONES, *pursuing her (both are playing, yet both have real anger).* You gimme boocoup now?

YEN. Boocoup what? I don't know what you want. Crazy GI, you dinky dow.

SGT. BRISBEY. *Pavlo!*

Yen, Pavlo, Jones, and Mamasan

PAVLO, *who is still putting on the fatigues.* I'm in the can, Brisbey.
I'll be there in a minute.

ARDELL. He be there, Brisbey.

JONES. You got lips as fat as mine, you know that, Ho?

YEN. Tôi không biêt.

JONES. Shit, you don't know.

YEN. Shit. I can say, too. I know. Shit.

(And he is reaching for her.)

No. We fini. Fini. You no talk me no more, you numba fuckin'
ten.

She bounces away to sit on a crate and look at sheet music.

SGT. BRISBEY. Do you know, Pavlo? I saw the metal point of that
mine sticking up from the ground just under my foot—I said,
"That's a mine. I'm stepping on a mine." And my foot went
right on down and I felt the pin sink and heard the first small
. . . pop. I jumped . . . like a fool. And up she came right outa
the ground. I hit at it with my hand as if to push it away, it
came up so slow against my hand. . . . Steel . . . bits . . . of
dirt . . .

PAVLO. I'm off duty now, Brisbey.

ARDELL. Ole Brisbey got himself hit by a Bouncin' Betty. That a
kind of land mine; you step on it, she jump up to about right
here *(indicating his waist).* . . . Then she blow you in half. That
why she got that name. Little yellow man dug a hole, put it in,
hoped he'd come around. He an old man, damn near; got seventeen years in the army; no legs no more, no balls, one arm.

*A small Vietnamese boy comes running by and grabs Pavlo's
hand.*

BOY. Hey, GI, show you numba one! *(He guides him into the
whorehouse-bar and leaves him there.)*

PAVLO, *to Jones, who is sitting there drinking a beer.* Hey, what's
goin' on?

JONES. What's happenin', man?

MAMASAN, *returning.* Hello, hello! You come my house, I am glad. Do you want a beer? I have. Do you want a girl? I have. Numba one girl. Numba one. You want?

PAVLO, *pointing to Mamasan.* You?

MAMASAN. No, no, I am Mamasan. But I have many girl. You see, maybe you like. Maybe you want short time, huh? Maybe you want long time. I don't know, you tell me. All numba one.

JONES—*laughs.* Man, don't you believe that ole lady, you just gotta get on and ride. *(Indicating Yen)* Like her. I been. And I'm restin' to go again; an' I don't think it any kinda numba one; but I been outa the world so *damn* long. I jus' close my eyes an' jive my own self—"That ain't no dead person," I say, "that ain't no dead Ho jus' 'cause she layin' so still. I saw her walk in here." I mean, man they so screwed up over here. They got no nature. You understand me, Bro? They got no nature, these women. You—how long you been over here?

PAVLO. Not long; couple a weeks.

JONES. You new then, huh?

PAVLO. Yeh.

JONES. You wanna go? *(Reaching out toward Yen, who is across the room, calling to her)* Hey, Ho! C'mon over here!

YEN. You talk me?

JONES. Yeh, Baby, you. C'mon over here. You wanna go, man?

PAVLO, *taking a seat.* What about the V.D.?

JONES—*big laugh.* What about it?

YEN, *approaching with a beer.* I no have. I no sick. No. No sweat, GI. You want short-time me, no sweat.

JONES. Shit, Ho, you insides rotten. You Vietnamee, ain't you? Vietnamee same-same V.D.

YEN. No! No sick! *(As Jones grabs her, sets her down on Pavlo's lap)* What you do? No.

JONES. I'm jus' tryin' ta help you get some money, Baby. I be you Sportsman. Okay. *(Holding her in place)* You just sit on down

an' be nice on the man's lap, pretty soon he ain't gonna be worried 'bout no V.D. If you jus' . . . sorta shift (*he demonstrates*)
every now and then. Okay. . . .

(*She is still now and he turns his attention to Pavlo.*)

Now, lemme tell you 'bout it, lemme tell you how it is. It be hot,
man. I come from Georgia, and it get hot in Georgia, but it ain't
ever been this kinda hot, am I lyin'? An' you gonna be here one
year, and that three hundred sixty-five days, so you gonna sweat.
Now do you think I'm lyin'?

Yen is touching Pavlo, rubbing under his shirt.

PAVLO. I ain't never sweat so much.

JONES. So that's what I'm sayin'. You gonna be here and you gonna
sweat. And you gonna be here and you gonna get V.D.! You worried about sweatin'? Ahhhhh. You grinnin'. So I see I have made
my meanin' clear.

(*Yen has been rubbing Pavlo's thigh.*)

How you feelin' now? She kinda nice, huh? She kinda soft and
nice.

PAVLO. Where you work?

JONES—*laughs.* Don't you be askin' me where I work. That ain't
what you wanna know. I gotta get you straight, my man, gotta
get outa here, buy myself some supplies. My ole mom all the
time tellin' me, "Don't you go near that PX. You get blown away
for sure. Them V.C.s gotta wanna get that PX." Ain't it a world
of trouble?

PAVLO, *to Yen.* What's your name?

YEN. Name me Yen.

PAVLO. Name me Pavlo. Pavlo.

YEN. Paaa-blo.

PAVLO. How much?

JONES. Lord, she says his name, he loves her.

YEN. You want short-time: I ask Mamasan.

But Mamasan has been watching.

MAMASAN, *approaching.* Okay. Okay. Yen numba one. I am happy. Five hundred P's.

JONES. Two hundred.

MAMASAN. She very beautiful.

JONES. Two fifty.

MAMASAN. Four hundred, can do. No sweat.

JONES. Mamasan, who you think you jivin'?

MAMASAN. Yen boocoup boy friend! She very love!

JONES. Two fifty.

MAMASAN, *to Pavlo.* Three hundred twenty. You, huh? Three hundred twenty.

JONES. Pavlo, give her three hundred; tell her things is tough at home, she don't know.

MAMASAN, *as Pavlo hands her the money.* No, no, I talk you three hundred twenty!

JONES. And I talk him three hundred, Mamasan, three hundred!

MAMASAN, *softly, whiny, to Pavlo.* GI, you be nice; you give Mamasan ten P's more. GI? Ten P's very easy you!

PAVLO, *to Jones.* How much *is* ten P's, man?

JONES. Eight cents, or about—

PAVLO. Eight cents! Eight cents. Over eight goddamn stupid cents I'm standin' here!

JONES *(as Pavlo is giving more money to Mamasan).* Man, no!

MAMASAN, *patting Pavlo on the back.* Okay, okay. You numba one—.

YEN, *taking Pavlo by the hand toward the bed.* I show you.

JONES, *as he leaves.* Oh man, deliver me from these green troops; they makin' everybody fat but me.

The whistle blows loudly, and the troops come roaring on and into formation, facing the tower.

SGT. TOWER. GEN'LMEN!

(And his voice stops Pavlo, who comes to attention kneeling on the bed. Yen has jumped onto the bed. As Sgt. Tower continues his speech, she unbuttons Pavlo's pants, unbuttons his shirt, takes his pants down—all this as Sgt. Tower gives instructions.)

(Holding up a rifle) This an M-sixteen rifle, this the best you country got. Now we got to make you good enough to have it. You got to have feelin' for it, like it a good woman to you, like it you arm, like it you rib. The command is "Right shoulder . . . *harms!*" At the command "harms," raise and carry the rifle diagonally across the body, at the same time grasping it at the balance with the left hand, trigger guard in the hollow of the bone. Then carry the left hand, thumb and fingers extended, to the small of the stock, and cut away smartly, and everything about . . . you, Trainee, is at the position of attention. RIGHT SHOULDER . . . HARMS!

THE MEN, *performing the drill (as Pavlo also yells and performs it in pantomime with them)*. ONE, TWO, THREE, FOUR.

SGT. TOWER. You got to love this rifle, Gen'lmen, like it you pecker and you love to make love. You got to care about how it is and what can it do and what can it not do, what do it want and need. ORDER HARMS!

THE MEN and PAVLO. ONE, TWO, THREE, FOUR.

SGT. TOWER. RIGHT SHOULDER . . . HARMS!

THE MEN and PAVLO. ONE, TWO, THREE, FOUR.

CORPORAL. FORWARD HARCH!

And Pavlo pulls up his trousers and marches.

SGT. TOWER. AIN'T NO USE IN GOIN' HOME . . .

THE MEN. AIN'T NO USE IN GOIN' HOME . . .

Pavlo's marching is joyous.

SGT. TOWER. JODY GOT YOUR GAL AND GONE . . .

THE MEN. JODY HUMPIN' ON AND ON.

Something of Pavlo's making love to Yen is in his marching.

SGT. TOWER. AIN'T NO USE IN GOIN' BACK . . .

THE MEN. JODY GOT OUR CADILLAC.

CORPORAL. LORD HAVE MERCY, I'M SO BLUE . . .

THE MEN. IT TWO MORE WEEKS TILL I BE THROUGH.

CORPORAL. Count cadence, delayed cadence, count cadence—count!

And the men, performing delayed cadence, exit. Pavlo counts with them, marching away beside the bed, around the bed, leaping upon the bed as the counting comes to its loud end.

SGT. BRISBEY *(who has been onstage in his bed all this while), calling.* Pavlo!

PAVLO. Just a second, Brisbey!

SGT. BRISBEY. Pavlo!

PAVLO, *crossing toward Brisbey.* Whatta you want, Brisbey?

SGT. BRISBEY. Pavlo, can I talk to you a little?

PAVLO. Sure.

SGT. BRISBEY. You're a medic, right?

PAVLO. Yeh.

SGT. BRISBEY. But you're not a conscientious objector, are you? So you got a rifle.

PAVLO. Sure.

Pavlo is busy now with Brisbey's pulse and chart, straightening the bed, preparing the shot he must give.

SGT. BRISBEY. I like the feel of 'em. I like to hold 'em.

PAVLO. I'm not gonna get my rifle for you, Brisbey.

SGT. BRISBEY. Just as a favor.

PAVLO. No.

SGT. BRISBEY. It's the only pleasure I got anymore.

PAVLO. Lemme give you a hypo; you got a visitor; you can see him before you sleep.

SGT. BRISBEY. The egg that slept, that's what I am. You think I look like an egg with a head?

(Pavlo is preparing the needle. There is a figure off in the shadows.)

Or else I'm a stump. Some guys, they get hit, they have a stump. I am a stump.

PAVLO. What about your visitor; you wanna see him?

And the figure, Sgt. Wall, steps forward. He is middle-aged, gray-haired, chunky.

SGT. BRISBEY. Henry?

SGT. WALL. It's me, Brisbey, how you doin'?

SGT. BRISBEY. Henry, Henry, who was the first man round the world, Henry? That's what I want to know. Where's the deepest pit in the ocean? You carryin'? What do you have? Forty-five? You must have a blade. Magellan. Threw out a rope. I ever tell you that story? Gonna go sleepy-bye. Been tryin' to get young Pavlo Hummel to put me away, but he prefers to break needles on me. How's the unit? You tell 'em I'll be back. You tell 'em, soon as I'm well, I'll be back.

SGT. WALL. I'm off the line . . . now, Brisbey. No more boonies. I'm in Supply now.

SGT. BRISBEY. Supply? What . . . do you supply? *(Slight pause, as if bewildered. Thinking, yet with bitterness)* If I promise to tell you the secret of life, Henry, will you slit my throat? You can do it while I'm sleeping.

PAVLO. Don't he just go on?

SGT. BRISBEY. Young Hummel here, tell him who you love. Dean Martin. Looks at ole Dino every chance he gets. And "Combat." Vic Morrow, man. Keeps thinkin' he's gonna see himself. Dino's cool, huh. Drunk all the time.

PAVLO. That's right.

SGT. BRISBEY. You fuckin' asshole. Henry. Listen. You ever think to yourself, "Oh, if only it wasn't Brisbey. I'd give anything. My own legs. Or one, anyway. Arms. Balls. Prick." Ever . . . Henry?

Silence.

SGT. WALL. No.

SGT. BRISBEY. Good. Don't. Because I have powers I never dreamed of and I'll hear you if you do, Henry, and I'll take them. I'll rip them off you.

Silence.

SGT. WALL. You'll be goin' home soon. I thought . . . we could plan to get together. . . .

SGT. BRISBEY. Right. Start a softball team.

SGT. WALL. Jesus Christ, Brisbey, ain't you ever gonna change? Ain't you ever gonna be serious about no—

SGT. BRISBEY. I have changed, Motherfucker. You blind or somethin' askin' me if I changed. You get the fuck outa here, hear me?

(Wall is leaving, having left a pint of whiskey.)

You take a tree, you cut off its limbs, whatta you got? You got a stump. A living feeling thinking stump.

PAVLO. You're not a tree, Brisbey.

SGT. BRISBEY. And what terrible cruelty is that? Do you know? There is responsibility. I want you to get me that rifle. To save you from the sin of cruelty, Pavlo.

(As Pavlo is moving with alcohol, cotton, to prepare the shot)

You are cruel, Pavlo . . . you and God. The both of you.

PAVLO. Lemme do this, man.

SGT. BRISBEY *(as Pavlo gives the shot).* Do you know . . . if you were to get the rifle, Pavlo, I'd shoot you first. It's how you'll end up anyway. I'd save you time. Get you home quicker. I know you, boy.

PAVLO. Shut up, man. Relax . . .

SGT. BRISBEY. You've made me hate you.

PAVLO. I'm sorry. I didn't mean that to happen.

SGT. BRISBEY. No, no, you're not sorry. You're not. You're glad it's me, you're glad it's not you. God's always glad that way because

Pavlo and Sergeant Brisbey

it's never him, it's always somebody else. Except that once. The only time we was ever gonna get him, he tried to con us into thinkin' we oughta let him go. Make it somebody else again. But we got through all that shit he was talkin' and hung on and got him good—fucked him up good—nailed him up good . . . just once . . . for all the billion times he got us.

PAVLO. Brisbey, sometimes I don't think you know what you're sayin'.

A captain enters upstage left, carrying clipboard.

CAPTAIN. Grennel.

GRENNEL, *appearing from the back, far upstage.* Yes, Sir.

CAPTAIN. Go get me Hummel. He's down with Brisbey.

SGT. BRISBEY. I keep thinkin', Pavlo, 'bout this kid got his hand blown off and he kept crawlin' round lookin' for his fingers. Couldn't go home without 'em, he said, he'd catch hell. No fingers.

(Pavlo shakes his head.)

I keep thinkin' about ole Magellan, sailin' round the world. Ever hear of him, Pavlo? So one day he wants to know how far under him to the bottom of the ocean. So he drops over all the rope he's got. Two hundred feet. It hangs down into the sea that must go down and down beyond its end for miles and tons of water. He's up there in the sun. He's got this little piece of rope danglin' from his fingers. He thinks because all the rope he's got can't touch bottom, he's over the deepest part of the ocean. He doesn't know the real question. How far beyond all the rope you got is the bottom?

PAVLO. Brisbey, I'm gonna tell you somethin'. I tried to kill myself once. Honest to God. And it's no good. You understand me. I don't know what I was thinkin' about. I mean, you understand it was a long time ago and I'd never been laid yet or done hardly anything, but I have since and it's fantastic. I just about blew this girl's head off, it was fantastic, but if I'd killed myself, it'd never a happened. You see what I'm sayin', Brisbey? Somethin' fantastic might be comin' to you.

GRENNEL, *entering.* Hummel. Man, the Captain wants to see you.

PAVLO. Captain Miller? Captain Miller!

He leaves.

SGT. BRISBEY. Pavlo!

GRENNEL, *as he wheels Brisbey off.* How you doin', Brisbey?

PAVLO, *rushing up to the captain, who stands with his clipboard.* Sir, PFC Hummel reporting as ordered.

CAPTAIN. Good afternoon, Hummel.

PAVLO. Good afternoon, Sir.

CAPTAIN. Are you smiling, Hummel?

PAVLO. Excuse me, Sir.

CAPTAIN. Your ten-forty-nine says you're not happy at all; it says you want a transfer out of this unit because you're ashamed to serve with us. I was wondering how could you be ashamed and smiling simultaneously, Hummel.

PAVLO. I don't know, Sir.

CAPTAIN. That's not a very good answer.

PAVLO. No, Sir.

CAPTAIN. Don't you think what you're doing here is important? You helped out with poor Brisbey, didn't you?

PAVLO. Yes, Sir.

CAPTAIN. That's my point, Hummel. There are people alive who would be dead if you hadn't done your job. Those invalids you care for, you feed them when they can't, you help them urinate, defecate, simple personal things they can't do for themselves but would die without. Have you asked any one of them if they think what you are doing is important or not, or if you should be ashamed?

PAVLO. Yes, Sir . . . more or less. But . . . I . . . just think I'd be better off in squad duty.

Distant firing and yelling are heard to which neither the captain nor Pavlo respond. There is a quality of echo to the gunfire; then there is a clattering and Parham, a young Negro PFC, appears at the opposite side of the stage in full combat gear except for his helmet, which is missing. He has come a few steps onto the stage. He crouches.

PARHAM. Damn, baby, why that ole sarge gotta pick on me?

PAVLO. I'm Regular Army, Sir; I'm going to extend my tour.

CAPTAIN. You like it here, Hummel?

PARHAM. Damn that ole sarge. I run across that field I get shot sure as hell. *(He breathes.)* Lemme count to five. Lemme do it on five.

CAPTAIN. How many days left in your tour, Hummel?

PARHAM. Lemme do it like track and field.

PAVLO. I enlisted because I wanted to be a soldier, Sir, and I'm not a soldier here. Four nights ago on perimeter guard, I tried to set up fields of fire with the other men in the bunker—do you know what I mean, Sir? Designating who would be responsible for what sector of terrain in case of an attack? And they laughed at me; they just sat on the bunker and talked all night and they didn't stay low and they didn't hide their cigarettes when they smoked or anything.

PARHAM. FIVE!

(And he runs no more than two steps before a loud explosion hits. He goes down, bounces, and rolls onto his back, slamming his fist into the ground in outrage.)

DAMNIT! I KNEW IT! I KNEW IT! I KNEW IT!

CAPTAIN. You want the V.C. to come here?

PAVLO. I want to feel, Sir, that I'm with a unit Victor Charlie considers valuable enough to want to get it. And I hope I don't have to kill anyone; and I hope I don't get killed.

PARHAM, *still trying but unable to rise.* Medic? Medic? Man, where you at? C'mon out here to me! Crawl on out here to me.

PAVLO. But maybe you can't understand what I'm saying, Sir, because you're an R.O.T.C. officer and not O.C.S., Sir.

CAPTAIN. You mean I'm not Regular Army, Hummel.

PAVLO. An R.O.T.C. officer and an O.C.S. officer are not the same thing.

CAPTAIN. Is that so, Hummel?

PAVLO. I think so, Sir.

CAPTAIN. You want to get killed, don't you, Hummel?

PAVLO. No, Sir. No.

CAPTAIN. And they will kill you, Hummel, if they get the chance. Do you believe that? That you will die if shot, or hit with shrapnel, that your arm can disappear into shreds, or your leg vanish— do you believe that, Hummel? That you can and will, if hit hard enough, gag and vomit and die . . . be buried and rot—do you believe yourself capable of that? . . .

PAVLO. Yes . . . Sir. I . . . do . . .

PARHAM. Nooooooo! (*Quick pause. He looks about.*) Ohhh, shit, somebody don't help me, Charlie gonna come in here, cut me up, man. He gonna do me.

CAPTAIN. All right, Hummel.

PARHAM. Oh, Lord, you get me outa here, I be good, man. I be good, no shit, Lord, I'm tellin' it.

CAPTAIN. All right . . . you're transferred. I'll fix it.

Pavlo salutes. The captain salutes, pivots, exits. Pavlo moves to change into combat gear, which he finds in a footlocker. He exits.

PARHAM. What's happenin'? I don't know what's happenin'!

(*And the light goes, and he is alone in the jungle, in a center of flickering silver. It is night, there are sounds.*)

Hummel, c'mon. It's me, man, Parham; and I ain't jivin', mister. I been shot. I been truly shot.

(*He pauses, breathing, raises his head to look down at himself.*)

Ohhhh, look at me; ohhh, look at my poor stomach. Ohhhh, look at me, look at me. Oh, baby, stop it, stop bleedin', stop it, stop it; you my stomach, I'm talkin' to you, I'm tellin' you what to do, YOU STOP IT!

(*His hands are pressing furiously on his stomach. And he lies for a moment in silence before shuddering and beginning again.*)

SOMEBODY GET ME A DUSTOFF! Dustoff control, do you hear me? This here PFC Jay Charles Johnson Parham. I am coordinates X-ray Tango Foxtrot . . . Lima. . . . Do you hear me? I hurtin', baby . . . hear me. Don't know what to do for myself . . . can't remember . . . don't know what it is gone wrong. . . . Requesting one med-evac chopper. . . . I am one litter patient, gun shot wounds, stomach. Area secure. C'mon hear me . . . this ole nigger . . . he gonna die.

Two Vietcong, appearing soundlessly, are suddenly upon him. One carries a rifle.

1ST V.C. Hello, GI.

PARHAM. Oh, no. Oh, no. No.

1ST V.C., *very singsong.* Okay. Okay.

2ND V.C. You numba one.

PARHAM. Get away from me! I talkin' to you, Charlie, you get away from me! You guys get away from me! MEDIC! ME—

They say, "Okay, okay," "You numba one." At a nod from the Vietcong with the weapon, his partner has jumped forward into a sitting position at Parham's head, one leg pinning down each shoulder, the hands grasping under his chin, stuffing a rag into his mouth. There are only the sounds of the struggle. The other Vietcong approaches and crouches over Parham, holding a knife over him. Parham stares, and his feet move slowly back and forth.

1ST V.C. Numba one, you can see, GI? Airplane me . . . Vietnam. Have many bomb. Can do boom-boom, you stand! (*He moves the knife up and down.*) Same-same you, many friends me, fini. Where airplane now, GI? Where Very gun?

(*And he places the blade against Parham's chest, and Parham behind his gag begins to howl, begins to flail his pinioned arms and beat his heels furiously upon the ground.*)

Okay, okay . . . ! Ông di dâu?

(Then the knife goes in and the Vietcong get up to stand over Parham, as he turns onto his side and pulls himself into a knot as if to protect himself, knees tight to his chest, arms over his head. They unbuckle his pistol belt, take his flak vest and billfold from his pocket, and are working at removing his shirt when they both straighten at a sound. They seize his fallen rifle and run to disappear. Pavlo appears, moving low, accompanied by Ryan.)

RYAN. Man, I'm tellin' you let's get outa here.

PAVLO, *pointing.* No, no. There. *(He has a circular belt hooked over his shoulder, and he moves toward the body.)* Just look.

(Ryan is following.)

Hey, man . . . hey . . . *(He rolls Parham over.)* Ohhhhh . . . look at him.

RYAN. It's Parham.

PAVLO. Man, he's all cut. . . .

RYAN. Pavlo, let's get outa here! *(And he starts to move off.)* What the hell's it matter?

PAVLO. I'll carry him.

RYAN, *as Pavlo hands him his rifle.* I ain't worried about who has to carry him, for chrissake, I wanna get outa here. *(On the move)* I'm gonna hustle over there to the side there.

PAVLO. Nooooooo . . .

RYAN. Give you some cover.

And Ryan is gone, leaving Pavlo with the body. The carrier's procedure, which Pavlo undertakes through the following speeches, is this: He places the circular belt under the dead man's buttocks, one length along his back, the other below and across his legs, so that two loops are formed, one on either side of the man. He then lies down with his back to the dead man and fits his arms through the two loops. He grasps the man's left arm with his own right hand and rolls to his right so that the man rolls with him and is on his back. He then rises to one knee, keeping the body pressed tightly to his own. As Pavlo begins this task, Ardell is there, appearing as Ryan departs.

ARDELL. How many that make?

PAVLO. What's that?

ARDELL. Whatta you think, man? Dead bodies!

PAVLO. Who the hell's countin'?

ARDELL. Looookeeeee. Gettin' ta *beeeee bad!*

PAVLO. This one's nothin'. When they been out here a couple a days, man, that's when it's interesting—you go to pick 'em up, they fall apart in you hands, man. They're mud—pink mud—like turnin' over a log, all maggots and ants. You see Ryan over there hidin' in the bushes. I ain't hidin' in no bushes. And Parham's glad about that. They're all glad. Nobody wants to think he's gonna be let lay out here.

ARDELL. Ain't you somethin'.

PAVLO. I'm diggin' it, man. Blowin' people away. Cuttin' 'em down. Got two this afternoon I saw and one I didn't even see—just heard him out there jabberin' away—*(and he makes a sound mimicking a Vietnamese speaking).* And I walked a good goddamn twenty rounds right over where it sounded like he was: he shut up his fuckin' face. It ain't no big thing.

ARDELL. Like bringin' down a deer . . . or dog.

PAVLO. Man, people's all I ever killed. Ohhhh, I feel you thinkin', "This poor boy don't know what he's doin'; don't know what he got into." But I do. I got a dead boy in my hands. In a jungle . . . the middle a the night. I got people maybe ten feet away, hidin'—they're gonna maybe cut me down the minute I move. And I'm gonna . . . *(During all this he has struggled to load the body like a pack on his back. Now he is rising. Is on his knee.)* . . . take this dead thing back and people are gonna look at me when I do it. They're gonna think I'm crazy and be glad I'm with 'em. I'm diggin'—

(And the first Vietcong comes streaking out from a hiding place.)

Ryan, Ryan, Ryan!

(And the Vietcong, without stopping, plunges the knife into Pavlo's side and flees off. Pavlo falls, unable, because of the body on his back, to protect himself.)

What happened?

ARDELL. The blood goin' out a hole in your guts, man; turn you into water.

PAVLO. He hit me. . . .

ARDELL. *Turn you into water!* Blood goin' in the brain make you think; in your heart make you move; in your prick makes you hard, makes you come. *You lettin' it drop all over the ground!*

PAVLO. I won't . . . I'll . . . noooooo. . . . *(Trying to free himself of the body)* Ryan . . .

ARDELL. The knowledge comin', baby. I'm talkin' about what your kidney know, not your fuckin' fool's head. I'm talkin' about your skin and what it sayin', thin as paper. We melt; we tear and rip apart. Membrane, baby. Cellophane. Ain't that some shit.

PAVLO. I'll lift my arm. *(But he can't.)*

ARDELL. Ain't that some shit.

PAVLO. Noooooo . . .

ARDELL. A bullet like this finger bigger than all your fuckin' life. Ain't this finger some shit.

PAVLO. RYAN.

ARDELL. I'm tellin' you.

PAVLO. Nooooo.

ARDELL. RYAN!

PAVLO. RYAN!

ARDELL *(as Ryan comes running on with a second soldier)*. Get on in here.

The two soldiers struggle to free Pavlo from the body, as Sgt. Tower comes striding on and mounts his platform. Pavlo, being dragged off by the soldiers, yells and yells.

PAVLO. Ryan, we tear. We rip apart. Ryan, we tear. *(He is gone.)*

SGT. TOWER. You gonna see some funny shit, Gen'lmen. You gonna see livin' breathin' people disappear. Walkin' talkin' buddies. And you gonna wanna kill and say their name. When you been in so many fights and you come out, you a survivor. It what you are and do. You survive.

As a body detail removes Parham.

ARDELL. Thin and frail.

SGT. TOWER. Gen'lmen, can you hear me?

ARDELL. Yes, Sergeant.

SGT. TOWER. I saw this rifle one time get blown right outa this boy's hands and him start wailin' and carryin' on right there how he ain't ever goin' back on no line; he'll die for sure, he don't have that one rifle in all the world. You listenin' to me, Gen'lmen? I'm gonna tell you now what you do when you lost and it black, black night. The North Star show you true north accurate all year round. You gonna see the Big Dipper and two stars on the end called the pointer and they where the water would come on outa that dipper if it had water in it, and straight out from there is this big damn star, and that the North Star, and once you know north you ain't lost no more!

And Pavlo has appeared, walking slowly as in a dream, looking at Sgt. Tower.

PAVLO. YES, SERGEANT!

An explosion hits, and Pavlo, yelling, goes down.

ARDELL. What you sayin'? Yes, Sergeant.

PAVLO, *struggling to rise.* YES, SERGEANT!

ARDELL. Ask him what about that grenade come flyin'? How come if you so cool, if you such a fox, you don't know nothin' to do with no grenade but stand there holdin' it—get your abdominal and groin area blown to shit.

PAVLO. I DON'T KNOW WHAT YOU'RE TALKING ABOUT!

ARDELL. You walkin' talkin' scar, what you think you made of?

PAVLO. I got my shit together.

ARDELL. HOW MANY TIMES YOU GONNA LET 'EM HIT YOU?

PAVLO. AS MANY AS THEY WANT.

ARDELL. That man up there a fool, Jim.

PAVLO. Shut up.

ARDELL. You ever seen any North Star in your life?

PAVLO, *on the move toward Yen, who is kneeling in the distance.* I seen a lot of people pointin'.

ARDELL. They a bunch a fools pointin' at the air. "Go this way, go that way."

PAVLO. I want her, man. I need her. *(He touches her.)*

ARDELL. Where you now? What you doin'?

PAVLO. I'm with her, man.

ARDELL. You . . . in . . . her . . .

PAVLO, *taking her blouse off.* . . . soon . . .

ARDELL. Why you there? . . .

PAVLO. I dunno. . . . Jus' wanna . . .

ARDELL. You jus' gonna ride. . . .

PAVLO. I jus' wanna . . .

ARDELL. There was one boy walkin' . . .

PAVLO, *seizing her, embracing her.* I know; don't talk no shit.

ARDELL. Walkin' . . . singin' . . . soft, some song to himself, thinkin' on mosquitoes and Coke and bug spray, until these bushes in front of him burst and his fine young legs broke in half like sticks. . . .

PAVLO, *rising, trying to get his trousers off.* Leave me alone!

ARDELL. At seven his tonsils been cut out; at twelve there's appendicitis. Now he's twenty and hurtin' and screamin' at his legs, and then the gun come back. It on a fixed traversing arc to tear his yellin' fuckin' head right off.

PAVLO. Good; it's Tanner; it's Weber. It's Smith and not Pavlo. Minneti, not Pavlo. Klaus and you. You motherfucker. But not Pavlo. Not ever.

ARDELL. You get a knife wound in the ribs.

PAVLO. It misses my heart. I'm clean.

ARDELL. You get shrapnel all up and down your back.

PAVLO. It's like a dozen fifteen bee stings, all up and down my back.

ARDELL. And there's people tellin' you you can go home if you wanna. It's your second wound. They're sayin' you can go home when you been hit twice and you don't even check. You wanna go back out, you're thinkin', get you one more gook, get you one more slopehead, make him know the reason why.

PAVLO, *whirling, scooping up a rifle.* That's right. They're killin' everybody. They're fuckin' killin' everybody! *(The rifle is aimed at Ardell.)*

ARDELL. Like it's gonna make a difference in the world, man, what you do; and somethin' made bad's gonna be all right with this one more you're gonna kill. Poor ole Ryan gets dinged round about Tay Ninh, so two weeks later in Phu Loi you blow away this goddamn farmer. . . .

A farmer, wearing Vietnamese work clothes and a conical hat, appears in the distance, waving.

FARMER. Okay, GI, okay.

ARDELL. And think you're addin' somethin' up.

PAVLO. I blew him to fuckin' smithereens. He's there at twenty yards, wavin'.

FARMER. Okay, GI, okay. *(He sways in the distance.)*

PAVLO, *yelling at the farmer.* DUNG LYE. DUNG LYE. *(This is "Stop" in Vietnamese.)*

ARDELL. You don't know he's got satchel charges.

PAVLO. I do.

ARDELL. You don't know what he's got under his clothes.

PAVLO. I do. He's got dynamite all under his clothes. And I shoot him.

(Gunshot, as Pavlo fires.)

I fuckin' shoot him. He's under me. I'm screamin' down at him. RYAN. RYAN. And he's lookin' up at me. His eyes squinted like he knows by my face what I'm sayin' matters to me so maybe it matters to him. And then, all of a sudden, see, he starts to holler and shout like he's crazy, and he's pointin' at his foot, so I shoot it. *(He fires again.)* I shoot his foot and then he's screamin' and tossin' all over the ground, so I shoot into his head. *(Fires.)* I shot his head. And I get hit again. I'm standin' there over him and I get fuckin' hit again. They keep fuckin' hittin' me.

(Explosion and Pavlo goes flying forward.)

I don't know where I'm at. In my head . . . it's like I'm twelve . . . a kid again. Ardell, it's going to happen to meeeeeee. *(He is crawling.)*

ARDELL. What do you want me to do?

PAVLO. I don't want to get hit anymore.

ARDELL. What do you want me to do?

PAVLO. Tell me.

ARDELL. He was shot . . . layin' down under you, what did you see?

PAVLO. What?

ARDELL. He was squirmin' down under you in that ditch, what did you see?

PAVLO. I saw the grass . . . his head . . .

ARDELL. Nooooooooooo.

PAVLO. Help me, I saw the grass, his head . . .

ARDELL. Don't you ever hear?

PAVLO. I want out, Ardell. I want out.

ARDELL. When you gonna hear me?

PAVLO. What are you tryin' to tell me? I saw blood . . . bits of brain . . .

ARDELL. Noooooooooooo!

PAVLO. The grass, the grass . . .

ARDELL. When you shot into his head, you hit into your own head, fool!

PAVLO. What? NOOOOOOOOOOOOOO!

ARDELL. IT WAS YOUR OWN.

PAVLO. NOOOOOOOOOOOO!

(As Ardell has turned to leave)

Don't leave me you sonofabitch, I don't know what you're saying!

(And Ardell has stopped, with his back turned, far upstage.)

JIVE MOTHERFUCKING BULLSHIT!

(And Ardell is leaving and gone.)

And I . . . stood . . . lookin' . . . down . . . at that black, black Hudson River. . . . There was stars in it. . . . I'm a twelve-year-old kid. . . . I remember. . . . *(He is turning toward Yen, who is kneeling, singing.)* I went out toward them . . . diving . . . down. . . . *(He is moving toward Yen, crawling.)* They'd said there was no current, but I was twisted in all that water, fighting to get up . . . all my air burning out, couldn't get no more . . . *(still moving toward Yen)* and I was going down, fighting to get down. I was all confused, you see, fighting to get down, thinking it was up. I hit sand. I pounded. I pounded the bottom. I thought the bottom was the top. Black. No air.

The officer enters, striding swiftly.

OFFICER. Yes!

He carries a clipboard, on which he writes as Pavlo runs up to him. Yen, though she remains kneeling, stops singing.

PAVLO. SIR! I've just been released from Ward Seventeen, gunshot wound in my side, and I've been ordered back to my unit, Second of the Sixteenth, First Division, and I don't think I should have to go. This is the third time I been hit. I been hit in the ribs and leg and back. . . . I think there should be more trainin' in duckin' and dodgin', Sir. I been hit by a knife, shrapnel, and bullets.

OFFICER. Could you get to the point?

PAVLO. That is the point. I want to know about this regulation sayin' you can go home after your second wounding?

OFFICER. Pardon, Hummel?

PAVLO. I been told there's this regulation you can go home after your second wound. When you been hit twice, you can go home.

OFFICER. Hummel, wouldn't you be home if you were eligible to be home?

PAVLO. I don't know, Sir; but I wanted to stay the first two times, so I don't know and I was told I had the option the second time to go home or not, but I never checked and if I passed it by, Sir, I'd like to go back and pick it up.

OFFICER. You didn't pass it by; there's no such regulation.

PAVLO. It was a sergeant who told me.

OFFICER. These orders are valid.

PAVLO. Could you check, Sir?

OFFICER. I'm an expert on regulations, Hummel. These orders are valid. You've earned the Purple Heart. Now, go on back and do your job.

Raising his hand to salute, he pivots, as Pavlo is about to salute.

ARDELL. No, no.

PAVLO. I do my job.

Sgt. Wall enters the bar, calling to Yen. He wears civilian clothes—slacks and a flowered, short-sleeved shirt. Yen moves quickly to the bar area, where she pets him and then moves to prepare a drink for him.

SGT. WALL. Come here, Pretty Piggy, we talk boocoup love, okay? Make plans go my home America.

YEN. Sao. (*Vietnamese for "Liar."*)

SGT. WALL. No lie.

SGT. TOWER, *atop his platform. (Pavlo standing before him).* Gen'l-men. *(In a mournful rage)* Lemme tell you what you do, the enemy got you, he all around you. You the prisoner. You lis-tenin', Gen'lmen?

ARDELL, *all despairing sarcasm.* Yes, Sergeant.

SGT. TOWER. You got to watch out for the enemy. He gonna try to make you feel alone and you got no friends but him. He gonna make you mean and afraid; then he gonna be nice. We had a case with them North Koreans, this group a American POWs, one of 'em was wounded so he cried all night. His buddies couldn't sleep. So one night his buddies picked him up, I'm tellin' you, they carried him out the door into that North Korean winter, they set him down in the snow, they lef' him there, went on back inside. They couldn't hear him screamin' the wind was so loud. They got their sleep. You got to watch out for the enemy.

Pavlo pivots, turning away from Sgt. Tower and into the bar, where Mamasan greets him. Yen is still with Sgt. Wall, who is taking a big drink.

MAMASAN. Paaablooooo . . . how you-you. I give you beer, okay?

PAVLO, *unmoving, rigid.* Mamasan, chow ba.

SGT. WALL—*having finished his drink, takes up as if in mid-sen-tence.* ". . . so who," he says, "was the first motherfucker to sail 'round the world? Not Vasco da Gama." I don't know what he's sayin'. "Who was the first motherfucker to measure the ocean?" *(He is loud and waving his arms.)* I don't know! He wasn't even asking. MAMASAN! MAMASAN! ONE BEER! ONE BEER, ONE SAIGON TEA! *(And he reaches now to take Yen's hand and tug her gently around to his side of the table, drawing her near to sit on his lap.)* Come here; sit down. No sao. Fini sao. Boocoup love, Co Yen. Boocoup love. *(His hand is on her breast, as she nibbles his ear.)*

YEN. I think you maybe papasan America. Have many babysan.

SGT. WALL. No . . . no.

YEN. I think you sao.

SGT. WALL. No lie, Yen. No wife America, no have babysan. Take you, okay?

PAVLO. Sarge!

(Sgt. Wall looks up to Pavlo.)

Listen, I don't have too much time; I got to go pretty soon. How long you gonna be talkin' shit to that poor girl? I mean, see, she's the whore I usually hit on. I'm a little anxious, I'd like to interrupt you, you gonna be at her all fuckin' night. I'll bring her back in half an hour.

SGT. WALL. Sorry about that. Sorry—

PAVLO. I didn't ask you was you sorry.

SGT. WALL. This little girl's my girl.

PAVLO. She's a whore, man—

SGT. WALL. We got a deal, see, see; and when I'm here, she stays with me.

PAVLO. You got a deal, huh?

SGT. WALL. You guessed it, PFC.

PAVLO. Well, maybe you shoulda checked with me, you shoulda conferred with me maybe before you figured that deal was sound.

SGT. WALL. You have been informed.

PAVLO. But you don't understand, Sarge. She's the only whore here who moves me.

SGT. WALL. My baby.

PAVLO. You rear-echelon asshole!

SGT. WALL, *beginning to rise.* What's that?

PAVLO. Where you think you are, the goddamn PX? This the garbage dump, man, and you don't tell me nothin' down here, let alone who I can hit on, who I can't hit on, you see what I'm sayin' to you, Fuckface.

YEN. Paablo . . . no, no . . .

PAVLO. You like this ole man?

YEN, *moving to face Pavlo and explain.* Can be nice, Paablo . . .

PAVLO. Old man. Papasan. Can do fuck-fuck maybe one time one week. Talk, talk. Talk. No can do boom-boom. PAPASAN. NUMBA FUCKIN' TEN!

YEN, *angry at his stupidity.* Shut up, Paablo. I do him. Fini him. Do you. Okay.

PAVLO. Shut up?

SGT. WALL. You heard her.

PAVLO. Shut up? *(His hand twisting in her hair)* I don't know who you think this bitch is, Sarge, but I'm gonna fuck her whoever you think she is. I'm gonna take her in behind those curtains and I'm gonna fuck her right side up and then maybe I'm gonna turn her over, get her in her asshole, you understand me? You don't like it you best come in pull me off.

SGT. WALL, *switchblade popping open in his hand.* I ain't gonna have to, Punk.

Pavlo kicks him squarely in the groin. He yells, falls.

PAVLO. The fuck you ain't. Hey . . . were you ready for that? Were you ready for that, ole man? *(Dragging him along the ground, shoving him)* Called crawlin', you gettin' the hang of it, you ole man. Get up, get up.

(And Sgt. Wall moans as Pavlo lifts him.)

I want you gone, you mother, you understand? I don't wanna see you no more. You gonna disappear. You are gonna vanish.

And he flings Sgt. Wall away. Wall staggers, falls, and Pavlo picks the knife off the floor, goes for a beer, as Sgt. Tower begins to speak.

SGT. TOWER. This is a grenade, Gen'lmen. M-twenty-six-A-two fragmentation, Five-point-five ounces, composition B, time fuse, thirteen feet a coiled wire inside it, like the inside a my fist a animal and I open it and that animal leap out to kill you. Do you know a hunk a paper flyin' fast enough cut you in half like a knife, and when this baby hit, fifteen meters in all directions,

ONE THOUSAND HUNKS A WIRE GOIN' FAST ENOUGH!

(Ardell enters, joining Pavlo, who celebrates)

PAVLO. Did I do it to him, Ardell? The triple Hummel? Got to be big and bad. A little shuffle. Did I ever tell you? Thirteen months a my life ago.

YEN. Paaaabloooo, boocoup love!

PAVLO. Thirteen months a my life ago.

(And Sgt. Wall, there in the corner, beginning to move, is pulling pin on a grenade.)

What she did, my ole lady, she called Joanna a slut and I threw kitty litter, screamin'—cat shit—"Happy Birthday!" She called that sweet church-goin' girl a whore. To be seen by her now, up tight with this odd-lookin' whore, feelin' good and tall, ready to bed down. Feelin'—

(And the grenade, thrown by Sgt. Wall, lands. Wall flees, as Pavlo drops to his knees, seizing the grenade. He looks up in awe at Ardell. The grenade is in his hands in his lap.)

Oh Christ!

And the explosion comes, loud; it is a storm going into darkness and changing lights. Silence. Body detail enters, as Ardell, looking at Pavlo lying there, begins to speak. The body detail will wrap Pavlo in a poncho, put him on a stretcher, carry him to Ardell.

ARDELL. He don't die right off. Take him four days, thirty-eight minutes. And he don't say nothin' to nobody in all that time. No words; he just kinda lay up and look, and when he die, he bitin' on his lower lip, I don't know why. So they take him, they put him in a blue rubber bag, zip it up tight, and haul him off to the morgue in the back of a quarter-ton, where he get stuck naked into the refrigerator 'long with the other boys killed that day and the beer and cheese and tuna and stuff the guys who work at the morgue keep in the refrigerator except when it inspection time. The bag get washed, hung out to dry on a line out back a the morgue. *(Slight pause.)* Then . . . lemme see, well, finally he get shipped home, and his mother cry a lot, and his brother get so depressed he gotta go out and lay his chippie he so damn depressed about it all. And Joanna, she read his name in the paper, she let out this little gasp and say to her husband across the table, "Jesus, Jimmy, I used to go with that boy. Oh, damn that war, why can't we have peace? I think I'll call his mother." Ain't it some kinda world? *(And he is laughing.)* Soooooooo . . . that about it. That about all I got to say. Am I right, Pavlo? Did I tell you true? You got anything to say? Oh, man, I know you do, you say it out.

(Slight pause as Ardell moves to uncover Pavlo.)

Man, you don't say it out, I don't wanna know you. Be cool as you wanna be, Pavlo! Beee cool; lemme hear you. . . . You tell it to me: what you think of the cause? What you think a gettin' your ass blown clean off a freedom's frontier? What you think a bein' R.A. Regular Army lifer?

PAVLO, *softly, with nearly embarrassed laughter.* Sheeeeee . . . ittttt. . . . Oh, lord . . . oh . . .

ARDELL. Ain't it what happened to you? Lemme hear it.

PAVLO. . . . Shit!

ARDELL. And what you think a all the "folks back home," sayin' you a victim . . . you a animal . . . you a fool. . . .

PAVLO. They shit!

ARDELL. Yeh, Baby; now I know you. It all shit.

PAVLO. It all shit!

ARDELL. You my man again.

PAVLO. It shit.

ARDELL. Lemme hear it! My *main* man.

PAVLO. SHIT!

ARDELL. Main motherfuckin' man.

PAVLO. OH, SHIT!

ARDELL. GO!

PAVLO. SHIT!

ARDELL. GET IT! GET IT!

PAVLO—*a howl into silence.* SHHHHHHHHHIIIIIIIIIITTTTTT-TTTTTTttttttttt!

(*And four men enter, carrying the aluminum box of a coffin, while two other men go across the back of the stage doing the drill, the marching and twirling rifles that were done at the end of Act One. They go now, however, in the opposite direction. The coffin is placed beside Pavlo.*)

ARDELL. That right. How you feel? You feel all right? You gotta get that stuff outa you, man. You body know that and you body smart; you don't get that outa you, it back up on you, man, poison you.

The four men are placing Pavlo in the coffin. There is no precision in anything they do. All is casual, daily work.

PAVLO. But . . . I . . . I'm dead!

The men turn and leave.

ARDELL. Real soon; got wings as big as streets; got large, large wings. (*Slight pause.*) You want me to talk shit to you? Man, sure, we siftin' things over. We in a bar, man, back home, we got good soft chairs, beer in our hands, go-go girls all around; one of 'em got her eye on you, 'nother one thinkin' little bit on me. You believe what I'm sayin'. You *home,* Pavlo. (*Pause.*) Now . . . you c'mon and you be with me. . . . We gonna do a little singin'. You be with me. (*Sings*) Saw some stockin's . . . on the street . . .

PAVLO, *faltering.* Saw some . . . stockin's . . . on . . . the street . . .

Slight pause.

ARDELL. . . . Wished I was . . . between those . . . feet . . .

PAVLO. Wished I was between those feet!

Slight pause.

ARDELL and PAVLO, *together.* Once a week, I get to town. They see me comin', they jus' lay down. . . .

ARDELL. Sergeant, Sergeant, can't you see . . .

PAVLO. Sergeant, Sergeant, can't you see . . .

ARDELL. All this misery's killin' . . . me . . .

PAVLO. All this misery's killin'—

And Ardell lets the coffin lid slam shut, cutting Pavlo off.

ARDELL. Ain't no matter what you do . . . Jody done it . . . all to you. . . .

(Slight pause. Ardell is backing away.)

Lift your heads and lift 'em high . . . Pavlo Hummel . . . passin' by . . .

Ardell disappears upstage. The coffin stands in real light.

AUTHOR'S NOTE

If the character of Pavlo Hummel does not have a certain eagerness and wide-eyed spontaneity, along with a true, real, and complete inability to grasp the implications of what he does, the play will not work as it can. Pavlo is in fact lost. He has, for a long time, no idea that he is lost. His own perceptions define the world. He never understands that he provokes Kress or anybody else. When in the furnace room he responds to Kress's having told him he has his head up his ass, there is no cleverness in his response. He meant it to be clever but could not manage the words. He must make do with less than the situation demands; yet he is proud of having come as close as he did and is sure his quip will do. There must be something of the clinical neurotic in what he is and does. Nor can he be a street kid: this is what he *is not*, but wants to be. He is from middle income. Even with no father and with the mother he has, he was raised among middle-class kids. He has romanticized the street-kid tough guy and hopes to find himself in that image. It is Pavlo's body that changes. His physical efficiency, even his mental efficiency increases, but real insight never comes. Toughness and cynicism replace open eagerness, but he will learn only that he is lost, not how, why, or even where. His talent is for leaping into the fire.

The Basic Training of Pavlo Hummel was first produced by Joseph Papp, May 20, 1971, at the New York Shakespeare Festival Public Theater, under the direction of Jeff Bleckner, with the following cast (listed in order of appearance):

PAVLO HUMMEL	William Atherton
YEN	Victoria Racimo
ARDELL	Albert Hall
SERGEANT TOWER	Joe Fields
CAPTAIN (ALL OFFICERS)	Edward Cannan
CORPORAL	Anthony R. Charnota
KRESS	Earl Hindman
PARKER	Peter Cameron
PIERCE	Robert Lehman
BURNS	Stephen Clarke
HENDRIX	D. Franklyn Lenthall
HINKLE	Edward Herrmann
RYAN	John Walter Davis
MICKEY	Frederick Coffin
VOICE OF MRS. SORRENTINO	Victoria Racimo
MRS. HUMMEL	Sloane Shelton
SERGEANT BRISBEY	Lee Wallace
JONES	Garrett Morris
SERGEANT WALL	John Benson
MAMASAN	Christal Kim
SMALL BOY	Hoshin Seki
GRENNEL	Tom Harris
PARHAM	Bob Delegall
FIRST VIETCONG	Hoshin Seki
SECOND VIETCONG	Victoria Racimo

Associate Producer, Bernard Gersten; set by David Mitchell; costumes by Theoni V. Aldredge; lighting by Martin Aronstein.

Sticks and Bones

For Tâm

CHARACTERS

Ozzie

Harriet

David

Rick

Zung (the Girl)

Father Donald

Sergeant Major

Time: Autumn
Place: The family home

ACT ONE

Place: the family home.

Darkness; silence. Slides appear on both sides of the stage: the first is a black-and-white medium close-up of a young man, mood and clothing of the early 1900s; he is lean, reasonably handsome, black hair parted in the center. Voices speak. They are slow and relaxed, with an improvisational quality.

1ST CHILD'S VOICE. Who zat?

MAN'S VOICE. Grandpa Jacob's father.

New slide: group photo, same era, eight or ten people, all ages.

2ND CHILD'S VOICE. Look at 'em all!

1ST CHILD'S VOICE. How come they're all so serious?

New slide: small boy, black hair, black knickers.

WOMAN'S VOICE. There's Grandpa Oswald as a little boy.

1ST CHILD'S VOICE. Grandpa?

New slide: different boy, same pose.

WOMAN'S VOICE. And that's his brother Thomas. He died real young.

MAN'S VOICE. Scarlet fever.

New slide: young girl, seventeen or eighteen.

And that's his sister Christina.

WOMAN'S VOICE. No, that's Grandma.

MAN'S VOICE. No.

WOMAN'S VOICE. Sure.

New slide: Ozzie and Harriet, young, 1940s era.

There's the two of them.

MAN'S VOICE. Mmmmm, you're right, because that's Grandpa.

New slide: two boys, five and nine years old.

WOMAN'S VOICE. The taller one's David, right?

New slide: color close-up of David from the last moment of the play, a stricken look.

1ST CHILD'S VOICE. What's that one?

MAN'S VOICE. Somebody sick.

1ST CHILD'S VOICE. Boy . . . !

New slide: color photo of Ozzie, Harriet, and Father Donald. Father Donald, wearing a gym suit, his back to the camera, stands holding a basketball in one hand. Ozzie and Harriet face him, one on either side.

2ND CHILD'S VOICE. Oh, look at that one!

MAN'S VOICE. That's a funny one, isn't it.

WOMAN'S VOICE. That's one—I bet somebody took it—they didn't know it was going to be taken.

There is a bright flash and the stage is immediately illuminated. The set is an American home, very modern, with a quality of brightness, green walls, green rug. Stairs lead up to a bedroom— not lighted now—with a hallway leading off to the rest of the upstairs beyond. There is naturalness, yet a sense of space and, oddly, a sense also that this room, these stairs belong in the gloss of an advertisement.

Downstage, a TV on wheels faces upstage, glowing, murmuring. Ozzie, Harriet, and Father Donald—a slightly rotund, serious man—are standing as they were in the slide last seen.

FATHER DONALD. A feel for it is the big thing. A feel for the ball. You know, I mean, bouncing it, dribbling it. You don't even look at it.

Phone rings.

OZZIE. I'll get it.

FATHER DONALD. You can do it, Harriet. Give it a try. *(He bounces the ball to Harriet.)*

OZZIE. Hello? . . .

FATHER DONALD *(as Harriet catches the ball).* That a girl.

HARRIET. Oh, Father . . .

OZZIE, *hanging up.* Nobody there.

FATHER DONALD. That's what I'm telling you. You gotta help kids. Keeps 'em outa trouble. We help. Organized sports activities; it does 'em a world a good. You know that. And they need you.

OZZIE. I was a track and field man. Miler. Dash man—I told you.

Phone rings.

FATHER DONALD. But this is basketball season. *(He moves toward Harriet and then the door, as Ozzie goes to the phone, says "Hello," then listens intently.)* You listen to me, you get that husband of yours out there to help us. It'll do him good. Tell him he'd be a good little guard. A play maker.

HARRIET. Oh, Father Donald, bless me.

FATHER DONALD. Of course. *(He blesses her, holding the ball under his left arm.)* Bye-bye.

HARRIET *(as Father Donald goes).* Good-bye, Father.

(And she turns to look for a moment at Ozzie on the phone.)

Why aren't you talking?

(Silence: she is looking at him.)

Ozzie, why aren't you talking?

OZZIE, *slowly lowering the phone.* They're gone. They hung up.

HARRIET. You didn't say a word. You said nothing.

OZZIE. I said my name.

HARRIET. What did they want?

OZZIE. I said hello.

HARRIET. Were they selling something—is that what they wanted?

OZZIE. No, no.

HARRIET. Well . . . who was it?

OZZIE. What?

HARRIET. What are we talking about?

OZZIE. The Government. It was . . . you know. . . .

HARRIET. Ozzie! *(In fear)* No!

OZZIE—*some weariness in him.* No, he's all right, he's coming home!

HARRIET. Why didn't you let me speak? Who was it?

OZZIE. No, no.

HARRIET. It was David.

OZZIE. No, somebody else. Some clerk. I don't know who.

HARRIET. You're lying.

OZZIE. No. There was just all this static—it was hard to hear. But he was coming home was part of it, and they had his records and papers but I couldn't talk to him directly even though he was right there, standing right there.

HARRIET. I don't understand.

OZZIE. That's what they said. . . . And he was fine and everything. And he wanted them to say hello for him. He'd lost some weight. He would be sent by truck. I could hear truck engines in the background—revving. They wanted to know my name. I told them.

HARRIET. No more?

OZZIE. They were very professional. Very brusque . . .

HARRIET. No more . . . at all? . . .

The front door opens and Rick comes in. And the door slams. He is young, seventeen. His hair is long and neat, with sideburns. His clothing is elaborate—very, very up to date. He carries a guitar on his shoulder.

RICK. Hi, Mom. Hi, Dad.

HARRIET. Hi, Rick.

OZZIE. Hi, Rick.

HARRIET. Ohhh, Ricky, Ricky, your brother's on his way home. David's coming home!

OZZIE. We just got a call.

RICK. Ohhh, boy!

HARRIET. Isn't that wonderful? Isn't it? Your father talked to him. Oh, I bet you're starving. Sit, sit.

OZZIE. I talked to *somebody*, Rick.

HARRIET. There's fudge and ice cream in the fridge; would you like that?

RICK. Oh, yeah, and could I have some soda?

(She is on her way to the kitchen, nodding.)

Wow, some news. I'm awful hungry.

OZZIE. Never had a doubt. A boy like that—if he leaves, he comes back.

RICK, *as he picks up a comic book.* How about me? What if I left?

OZZIE. Absolutely. Absolutely.

(Silence. Rick reads the comic.)

I built jeeps . . . tanks, trucks.

RICK. What?

OZZIE. In the other war, I mean. Number Two. I worked on vehicles. Vehicles were needed and I worked to build them. Sometimes I put on wheels, tightened 'em up. I never . . . served . . . is what I mean. *(Slight pause.)* They got all those people—soldiers, Rick—you see what I mean? They get 'em across the ocean, they don't have any jeeps or tanks or trucks, what are they gonna do, stand around? Wait for a bus on the beachhead? Call a cab?

RICK. No public transportation in a war.

OZZIE. That's right, that's right.

Harriet enters, carrying fudge and ice cream.

HARRIET. Oh, Ozzie, Ozzie, do you remember—I just remembered that time David locked himself in that old icebox. We didn't know where he was. We looked all over. We couldn't find him. And then there was this icebox in this clearing . . . out in the middle. I'll bet you don't even remember.

OZZIE. Of course I remember.

HARRIET. And he leaped to us. So frightened.

OZZIE. He couldn't even speak—he couldn't even speak—just these noises.

HARRIET. Or that time he fell from that tree.

OZZIE. My God, he was somethin'! If he wasn't fallin', he was gettin' hit.

HARRIET. And then there was that day we went out into the woods. It was just all wind and clouds. We sailed a kite!

OZZIE. I'd nearly forgotten! . . .

RICK. Where was I?

HARRIET. You were just a baby, Rick. We had a picnic.

RICK. I'm gonna get some more soda, okay?

Harriet touches him as he passes.

OZZIE. What a day that was. I felt great that day.

HARRIET. And then Hank came along. Hank Grenweller. He came from out of the woods calling that—

OZZIE. That's right.

HARRIET. He was happy.

OZZIE. We were all happy. Except he'd come to tell us he was going away, leaving. And then we had that race. Wasn't that the day?

HARRIET. I don't remember.

OZZIE. Hank and me! Hank Grenweller. A foot race. And I beat him. I did it; got him.

HARRIET. Noooo.

OZZIE. It was only inches, but—

HARRIET. Ozzie, he took it easy. He wasn't trying.

OZZIE. He had to do his very best. Always. Never less. That was one thing you knew—no matter what he did or said, it was meant and true. All those long talks. Do you ever miss him?

HARRIET. He was a fine strong man.

OZZIE. I don't know why he left.

HARRIET. Do you remember when he showed us this house?

OZZIE. I remember when he showed me you.

HARRIET. You know that's not true. If it was close—and it was— that race you ran— *(This is not loud: there is intimacy; they are near one another.)* I remember now—it was because he let it be —no other reason. We were all having fun. He didn't want to make you feel badly. He didn't want to ruin all the fun. You know that. You know you do.

RICK, *calling from the kitchen.* You people want some fudge?

HARRIET. No, Rick.

OZZIE. I don't know he didn't try. I don't know that. *(He stares at Harriet.)*

HARRIET. I think I'll be going up to bed; take a little nap.

RICK. Sleepy, Mom?

HARRIET. A little. *(She is crossing toward Ozzie.)*

RICK. That's a good idea then.

HARRIET. Call me.

RICK. Okay.

HARRIET. Do you know, the day he left? It was a winter day. November, Ozzie. *(She moves toward the stairs.)*

OZZIE. I know.

HARRIET. I prayed; did you know that? Now he's home.

OZZIE. It was a winter day.

HARRIET, *at the top of the stairs.* I know.

RICK, *toying with his guitar.* Night, Mom.

(She doesn't answer but disappears down the hall. He looks up and yells after her.)

Night, Mom!

HARRIET, *from off.* Turn off the TV, somebody.

Rick crosses to the TV. He turns it off and wheels it back under the stairs. Ozzie watches. Silence.

OZZIE. I knew she was praying. She moves her lips.

(Rick does not look up. He begins, softly, to strum and tune the guitar.)

And something else—yes, sir, boy, oh, boy, I tell you, huh? What a day, huh? *(Slight pause.)* They got seventeen hundred million men they gotta deal with, how they gonna do that without any trucks and tanks and jeeps? But I'm some kinda jerk because I wasn't out there blastin' away, huh? I was useful. I put my time to use. I been in fights. Fat Kramer. . . . How we used to fight!

(Rick strums some notes on the guitar. Ozzie stares at him.)

How come I'm restless? I . . . seen him do some awful, awful things, ole Dave. He was a mean . . . foul-tempered little baby. I'm only glad I was *here* when they sent him off to do his killing. That's right. *(Silence.)* I feel like I swallowed ants, that's how restless I am. Outran a bowlin' ball one time. These guys bet me I couldn't do it and I did, beat it to the pins. Got a runnin' start, then the—

(A faint, strange rapping sound has stopped him, spun him around.)

Did you do that?

RICK. Somebody knockin'.

OZZIE. Knockin'?

RICK. The door, Dad.

OZZIE. Oh.

RICK. You want me to get it?

OZZIE. No, no. It's just so late. *(He moves for the door.)*

RICK. That's all right.

OZZIE. Sure.

He opens the door just a crack, as if to stick his head around. But the door is thrust open and a man enters abruptly. He is black or of Spanish descent, and is dressed in the uniform of a sergeant major and wearing many campaign ribbons.

SGT. MAJOR. Excuse me. Listen to me. I'd like to speak to the father here. I'd like to know who . . . is the father? Could . . . you tell me the address?

OZZIE. May I ask who it is who's asking?

SGT. MAJOR. I am. I'm asking. What's the address of this house?

OZZIE. But I mean, who is it that wants to know?

SGT. MAJOR. We called; we spoke. Is this seven-seventeen Dunbar?

OZZIE. Yes.

SGT. MAJOR. What's wrong with you?

OZZIE. Don't you worry about me.

SGT. MAJOR. I have your son.

OZZIE. What?

SGT. MAJOR. Your son.

OZZIE. No.

SGT. MAJOR. But he is. I have papers, pictures, prints. I know your blood and his. This is the right address. Please. Excuse me. (*He pivots, reaches out into the dark.*) I am very busy. I have your father, David.

He draws David in—a tall, thin boy, blond and, in the shadows, wearing sunglasses and a uniform of dress greens. In his right hand is a long, white, red-tipped cane. He moves, probing the air, as the sergeant major moves him past Ozzie toward the couch, where he will sit the boy down like a parcel.

OZZIE. Dave? . . .

SGT. MAJOR. He's blind.

OZZIE. What?

SGT. MAJOR. Blind.

OZZIE. I don't . . . understand.

SGT. MAJOR. We're very sorry.

OZZIE, *realizing.* Ohhhhh. Yes. Ohhhh. I see . . . sure. I mean, we didn't know. Nobody said it. I mean, sure, Dave, sure; it's all right—don't you worry. Rick's here, too, Dave—Rick, your brother, tell him hello.

RICK. Hi, Dave.

DAVID, *worried.* You said . . . "father."

OZZIE. Well . . . there's two of us, Dave; two.

DAVID. Sergeant, you said "home." I don't think so.

OZZIE. Dave, sure.

DAVID. It doesn't feel right.

OZZIE. But it is, Dave—me and Rick—Dad and Rick. Harriet! (*Calling up the stairs*) Harriet!

DAVID. Let me touch their faces. . . . I can't see. (*Rising, his fear increasing*) Let me put my fingers on their faces.

OZZIE, *hurt, startled.* What? Do what?

SGT. MAJOR. Will that be all right if he does that?

OZZIE. Sure. . . . Sure. . . . Fine.

SGT. MAJOR, *helping David to Ozzie.* It will take him time.

OZZIE. That's normal and to be expected. I'm not surprised. Not at all. We figured on this. Sure, we did. Didn't we, Rick?

RICK, *occupied with his camera, an Instamatic.* I wanna take some pictures, okay? How are you, Dave?

DAVID. What room is this?

OZZIE. Middle room, Dave. TV room. TV's in—

HARRIET, *on the stairs.* David! . . . Oh, David! . . . David . . .

And Ozzie, leaving David, hurries toward the stairs and looks up at her as she falters, stops, stares. Rick, moving near, snaps a picture of her.

The Sergeant Major, David, Harriet, Ozzie, and Rick

OZZIE. Harriet . . . don't be upset. . . . They say . . . Harriet, Harriet . . . he can't see! . . . Harriet . . . they say—he—can't . . . see. That man.

HARRIET, *standing very still.* Can't see? What do you mean?

SGT. MAJOR. He's blind.

HARRIET. No. Who says? No, no.

OZZIE. Look at him. He looks so old. But it's nothing, Harriet, I'm sure.

SGT. MAJOR. I hope you people understand.

OZZIE. It's probably just how he's tired from his long trip.

HARRIET, *moving toward him.* Oh, you're home now, David.

SGT. MAJOR, *with a large sheet of paper waving in his hands.* Who's gonna sign this for me, Mister? It's a shipping receipt. I got to have somebody's signature to show you got him. I got to have somebody's name on the paper.

OZZIE. Let me. All right?

SGT. MAJOR. Just here and here, you see? Your name or mark three times.

As they move toward a table and away from Harriet, who is near David.

OZZIE. Fine, listen, would you like some refreshments?

SGT. MAJOR. No.

OZZIE. I mean while I do this. Cake and coffee. Of course, you do.

SGT. MAJOR. No.

OZZIE. Sure.

SGT. MAJOR. No. I haven't time. I've got to get going. I've got trucks out there backed up for blocks. Other boys. I got to get on to Chicago, and some of them to Denver and Cleveland, Reno, New Orleans, Boston, Trenton, Watts, Atlanta. And when I get back they'll be layin' all over the grass; layin' there in pieces all over the grass, their backs been broken, their brains jellied, their insides turned into garbage. One-legged boys and no-legged boys.

I'm due in Harlem; I got to get to the Bronx and Queens, Cincinnati, Saint Louis, Reading. I don't have time for coffee. I got deliveries to make all across this country.

DAVID, *with Harriet, his hands on her face, a kind of realization.* Nooooooo. . . . Sergeant . . . nooo; there's something wrong; it all feels wrong. Where are you? Are you here? I don't know these people!

SGT. MAJOR. That's natural, Soldier; it's natural you feel that way.

DAVID. Nooooo.

HARRIET, *attempting to guide him back to a chair.* David, just sit, be still.

DAVID. Don't you hear me?

OZZIE. Harriet, calm him.

DAVID. The air is wrong; the smells and sounds, the wind.

HARRIET. David, please, please. What is it? Be still. Please . . .

DAVID. GODDAMN YOU, SERGEANT, I AM LONELY HERE! I AM LONELY!

SGT. MAJOR. I got to go. (*And he pivots to leave.*)

DAVID, *following the sound of the sergeant major's voice.* Sergeant!

SGT. MAJOR, *whirling, bellowing.* You shut up. You piss-ass soldier, you shut the fuck up!

OZZIE, *walking to the sergeant major, putting his hand on the man's shoulder.* Listen, let me walk you to the door. All right? I'd like to take a look at that truck of yours. All right?

SGT. MAJOR. There's more than one.

OZZIE. Fine.

SGT. MAJOR. It's a convoy.

OZZIE. Good.

They exit, slamming the door, and Rick, running close behind them, pops it open, leaps out. He calls from off.

RICK. Sure are lots a trucks, Mom!

HARRIET, *as he re-enters.* Are there?

RICK. Oh, yeah. Gonna rain some more too. (*And turning, he runs up the stairs.*) See you in the morning. Night, Dave.

HARRIET. It's so good to have you here again; so good to see you. You look . . . just . . .

(*Ozzie has slipped back into the room behind her, he stands, looking.*)

fine. You look—

(*She senses Ozzie's presence, turns, immediately, speaking.*)

He bewilders you, doesn't he?

(*And Ozzie, jauntily, heads for the stairs.*)

Where are you going?

(*He stops; he doesn't know. And she is happily sad now as she speaks—sad for poor Ozzie and David, they are so whimsical, so childlike.*)

You thought you knew what was right, all those years, teaching him sports and fighting. Do you understand what I'm trying to say? A mother knows *things* . . . a father cannot ever know them. The measles, smallpox, cuts and bruises. Never have you come upon him in the night as he lay awake and staring . . . praying.

OZZIE. I saw him put a knife through the skin of a cat. I saw him cut the belly open.

DAVID. Noooo. . . .

HARRIET, *moving toward him in response.* David, David. . . .

DAVID. Ricky!

(*There is a kind of accusation in this as if he were saying Ricky did the killing of the cat. He says it loudly and directly into her face.*)

HARRIET. He's gone to bed.

DAVID. I want to leave.

There is furniture around him; he is caged. He pokes with his cane.

HARRIET. What is it?

DAVID. Help me. (*He crashes.*)

OZZIE. Settle down! Relax.

DAVID. I want to leave! I want to leave! I want to leave. I . . .

(And he smashes into the stairs, goes down, flails, pounding his cane.)

want to leave.

OZZIE AND HARRIET. Dave! David! Davey!

DAVID. . . . to leave! Please.

He is on the floor, breathing. Long, long silence in which they look at him sadly, until Harriet announces the problem's solution.

HARRIET. Ozzie, get him some medicine. Get him some Ezy Sleep.

OZZIE. Good idea.

HARRIET. It's in the medicine cabinet; a little blue bottle, little pink pills.

(And when Ozzie is gone up the stairs, there is quiet. She stands over David.)

It'll give you the sleep you need, Dave—the sleep you remember. You're our child and you're home. Our good . . . beautiful boy.

And front door bursts open. There is a small girl in the doorway, an Asian girl. She wears the Vietnamese ao dai, *black slacks and white tunic slit up the sides. Slowly, she enters, carrying before her a small straw hat. Harriet is looking at the open door.*

HARRIET. What an awful . . . wind. (*She shuts the door.*)

Blackout. Guitar music.

A match flickers as Harriet lights a candle in the night. And the girl silently moves from before the door across the floor to the stairs, where she sits, as Harriet moves toward the stairs and Ozzie, asleep sitting up in a chair, stirs.

HARRIET. Oh! I didn't mean to wake you. I lit a candle so I wouldn't wake you.

(He stares at her.)

I'm sorry.

OZZIE. I wasn't sleeping.

HARRIET. I thought you were.

OZZIE. Couldn't. Tried. Couldn't. Thinking. Thoughts running very fast. Trying to remember the night David . . . was made. Do you understand me? I don't know why. But the feeling in me that I had to figure something out and if only I could remember that night . . . the mood . . . I would be able. You're . . . shaking your head.

HARRIET. I don't understand.

OZZIE. No.

HARRIET. Good night.

(She turns and leaves Ozzie sitting there, gazing at the dark. Arriving at David's door, she raps softly and then opens the door. David is lying unmoving on the bed. She speaks to him.)

I heard you call.

DAVID. What?

HARRIET. I heard you call.

DAVID. I didn't.

HARRIET. Would you like a glass of warm milk?

DAVID. I was sleeping.

HARRIET, *after a slight pause.* How about that milk? Would you like some milk?

DAVID. I didn't call. I was sleeping.

HARRIET. I'll bet you're glad you didn't bring her back. Their skins are yellow, aren't they?

DAVID. What?

HARRIET. You're troubled, warm milk would help. Do you pray at all any more? If I were to pray now, would you pray with me?

DAVID. What . . . do you want?

HARRIET. They eat the flesh of dogs.

DAVID. I know. I've seen them.

HARRIET. Pray with me; pray.

DAVID. What . . . do . . . you want?

HARRIET. Just to talk, that's all. Just to know that you're home and safe again. Nothing else; only that we're all together, a family. You must be exhausted. Don't worry; sleep. (*She is backing into the hallway. In a whisper*) Good night.

(*She blows out the candle and is gone, moving down the hall. Meanwhile the girl is stirring, rising, climbing from the living room up toward David's room, which she enters, moving through a wall, and David sits up.*)

DAVID. Who's there?

(*As she drifts by, he waves the cane at the air.*)

Zung? (*He stands.*) Chào, Cô Zung.

(*He moves for the door, which he opens, and steps into the hall, leaving her behind him in the room.*)

Zung. Chào, Cô Zung.

(*And he moves off up the hallway. She follows*)

Zung! . . .

Blackout. Music.

Lights up. It is a bright afternoon, and Ozzie is under the stairs with a screwdriver in his hand, poking about at the TV set.

OZZIE. C'mon, c'mon. Ohhhh, c'mon, this one more game and ole State's Bowl-bound. C'mon, what is it? Ohhh, hey . . . ohhhhh. . . .

HARRIET, *entering from the kitchen carrying a tray with a bowl of soup and a glass of juice.* Ozzie, take this up to David; make him eat it.

OZZIE. Harriet, the TV is broke.

HARRIET. What?

OZZIE. There's a picture but no sound. I don't—

Grabbing her by the arm, he pulls her toward a place before the set.

HARRIET. Stoppit, you're spilling the soup. *(She pulls free.)*

OZZIE. It's Sunday. I want to watch it. I turned it on, picture came on just like normal. I got the volume up full blast.

(Having set the tray down, Harriet now shoves the TV set deeper under the stairs, deeper into the place where it is kept when not in use.)

Hey! I want to watch it!

HARRIET. I want to talk about David.

OZZIE. David's all right.

(He turns, crosses toward the phone, picks up the phone book.)

I'm gonna call the repairman.

HARRIET, *following him.* Ozzie, he won't eat. He just lays there. I offer him food, he won't eat it. No, no. The TV repairman won't help, you silly. *(She takes the phone book from him.)* He doesn't matter. There's something wrong with David. He's been home days and days and still he speaks only when spoken to; there's no light in his eye, no smile; he's not happy to be here and not once has he touched me or held me, nor has he even shaken your hand.

Ozzie flops down in a chair.

OZZIE. Oh, I don't mind that. Why should I mind—

HARRIET. And now he's talking to himself! What about that? Do you mind that? He mutters in his sleep.

OZZIE, *exasperated.* Ohhhhhh.

HARRIET. Yes. And it's not a regular kind of talking at all. It's very strange—very spooky.

OZZIE. Spooky?

HARRIET. That's right.

OZZIE. I never heard him.

HARRIET. You sleep too deeply. I took a candle and followed. I was in his room. He lay there, speaking.

OZZIE. Speaking what?

HARRIET. I don't know. I couldn't understand.

OZZIE. Was it words?

HARRIET. All kind of funny and fast.

OZZIE. Maybe prayer; praying.

HARRIET. No. No, it was secret. Oh, Ozzie, I know praying when I hear it and it wasn't praying he was doing. We meant our son to be so different—I don't understand—good and strong. And yet . . . perhaps he is. But there are moments when I see him . . . hiding . . . in that bed behind those awful glasses, and I see the chalkiness that's come into—

OZZIE, *headed for the kitchen, looking for juice to drink.* Those glasses are simply to ease his discomfort.

HARRIET. I hate them.

OZZIE. They're tinted glass and plastic. Don't be so damn suspicious.

HARRIET. I'm not, I'm not. It's seeing I'm doing, not suspicion. Suspicion hasn't any reasons. It's you—now accusing me for no reason when I'm only worried.

OZZIE, *returning from the kitchen, angered.* Where's my juice?

HARRIET. I want to talk.

OZZIE. The hell with David for a minute—I want some juice.

HARRIET. Shut up. You're selfish. You're so selfish.

OZZIE, *walking to the tray and juice, attempting to threaten her.* I'll pour it on the floor. I'll break the glass.

She turns to move to get the juice.

HARRIET. A few years ago you might have done that kind of thing.

OZZIE. I woke up this morning, I could see so clearly the lovely way you looked when you were young. Beside me this morning, you were having trouble breathing. You kept . . . trying . . . to breathe.

(She approaches him to hand him the juice.)

What do you give me when you give me this?

HARRIET. I always looked pretty much as I do now. I never looked so different at all.

David appears from off upstairs, dressed in a red robe, and descends toward them.

DAVID, *sounding happy, yet moving with urgency.* Good morning.

OZZIE. Oh, David! Ohhh, good morning. Hello. How do you feel this fine bright morning; how do you feel?

DAVID. He was a big man, wasn't he?

OZZIE. What?

DAVID. Hank. You were talking about Hank Grenweller. I thought you were.

OZZIE. Oh, yes. Hank. Very big. Big. A good fine friend, ole Hank.

DAVID. You felt when he was with you he filled the room.

OZZIE. It was the way he talked that did that. He boomed. His voice just boomed.

DAVID. He was here once and you wanted me to sit on his lap, isn't that right? It was after dinner. He was in a chair in the corner.

HARRIET. That's right.

DAVID. His hand was gone—the bone showed in the skin.

OZZIE. My God, what a memory—did you hear that, Harriet? You were only four or five. He'd just had this terrible, awful auto accident. His hand was hurt, not gone.

DAVID. No. It was congenital and none of us knew.

OZZIE. What?

DAVID. That hand. The sickness in it.

OZZIE. Congenital?

DAVID. Yes.

OZZIE. What do you mean? What do you think you mean?

DAVID. I'd like some coffee.

He is seated now, but not without tension.

OZZIE. Hank's parents were good fine people, David.

DAVID. I know.

OZZIE. Well, what are you saying then?

DAVID. I'd like that coffee.

HARRIET. Of course. And what else with it?

DAVID. Nothing.

HARRIET. Oh, no, no, you've got to eat. To get back your strength. You must. Pancakes? How do pancakes sound? Or wheat cakes? Or there's eggs? And juice? Orange or prune: or waffles. I bet it's eggs you want. Over, David? Over easy? Scrambled?

DAVID. I'm only thirsty.

HARRIET. Well, all right then, coffee is what you'll have and I'll just put some eggs on the side; you used to love them so; remember?

And, picking up the tray, she is off toward the kitchen. There is a pause.

OZZIE. I mean, I hate to harp on a thing, but I just think you're way off base on Hank, Dave. I just think you're dead wrong.

DAVID. He told me.

OZZIE. Who?

DAVID. Hank.

OZZIE. You . . . talked to Hank?

DAVID. In California. The day before they shipped me overseas.

OZZIE. No, no. He went to Georgia when he left here. We have all his letters postmarked Georgia.

DAVID, *with great urgency.* It was California, I'm telling you. I was in the barracks. The C.Q. came to tell me there was someone to see me. It was Hank asking did I remember him? He'd seen my name on a list and wondered if I was Ozzie's boy. He was dying, he said. The sickness was congenital. We had a long, long talk.

OZZIE. But his parents were good fine people, David.

DAVID. Don't you understand? We spoke. Why did you make me think him perfect? It was starting in his face the way it started in his hand.

OZZIE. Oh! I didn't realize—I didn't know. You weren't blind. You could see. I didn't realize, Dave.

DAVID. What?

OZZIE. Did he wanna know about me? Did he mention me?

DAVID, *after thinking a moment.* He asked . . . how you were.

OZZIE. Well, I'm fine. Sure. You told him.

HARRIET, *entering with a cup of coffee.* It must be so wonderful for you to be home. It must just be so wonderful. A little strange, maybe . . . just a little, but time will take care of all that. It always does. You get sick and you don't know how you're going to get better and then you do. You just do. You must have terrible, awful, ugly dreams, though.

Slight pause.

OZZIE. She said you probably have terrible, awful, ugly dreams . . . though.

DAVID. What?

HARRIET. Don't you remember when we spoke last night?

DAVID. Who?

HARRIET. You called to me and then you claimed you hadn't.

DAVID. I didn't.

HARRIET. Ohhh, we had a lovely conversation, David. Of course you called. You called; we talked. We talked and laughed and it was very pleasant. Could I see behind your glasses?

DAVID. What? *(Moving away, crossing in flight from them)* Do . . . what?

HARRIET. See behind your glasses; see your eyes.

OZZIE. Me too, Dave; could we?

DAVID. My eyes . . . are ugly.

OZZIE. We don't mind.

HARRIET. We're your parents, David.

DAVID. I think it better if you don't.

OZZIE. And something else I've been meaning to ask you—why did you cry out against us that first night—to that stranger, I mean, that sergeant?

HARRIET. And you do dream. You do.

OZZIE. Sure. You needn't be ashamed.

HARRIET. We all do it. All of us.

OZZIE. We have things that haunt us.

HARRIET. And it would mean nothing at all—it would be of no consequence at all—if only you didn't speak.

DAVID. I don't understand.

OZZIE. She says she heard you, Dave.

HARRIET. I stood outside your door.

DAVID. No.

OZZIE. A terrible experience for her, Dave; you can see that.

HARRIET. Whatever it is, David, tell us.

OZZIE. What's wrong?

DAVID. No.

HARRIET. We'll work it out.

OZZIE. You can't know how you hurt us.

DAVID. I wasn't asleep.

OZZIE. Not until you have children of your own.

HARRIET. What?

(*Silence.*)

Not . . . asleep? . . .

DAVID. I was awake; lying awake and speaking.

OZZIE. Now wait a minute.

DAVID. Someone was with me—there in the dark—I don't know what's wrong with me.

HARRIET. It was me. I was with you. There's nothing wrong with you.

DAVID. No. In my room. I could feel it.

HARRIET. I was there.

And they have him cornered in another chair.

DAVID. No.

OZZIE. Harriet, wait!

HARRIET. What are you saying, "Wait"? I was there.

OZZIE. Oh, my God. Oh, Christ, of course. Oh, Dave, forgive us.

HARRIET. What?

OZZIE. Dave, I understand. It's buddies left behind.

DAVID. No.

OZZIE. But I do. Maybe your mother can't but I can. Men serving together in war, it's a powerful thing—and I don't mean to sound like I think I know it—all of it, I mean—I don't, I couldn't—but I respect you having had it—I almost envy you having had it, Dave. I mean . . . true comradeship.

DAVID. Dad . . .

OZZIE. I had just a taste—not that those trucks and factory were any battlefield, but there was a taste of it there—in the jokes we told and the way we saw each other first in the morning. We told dirty, filthy jokes, Dave. We shot pool, played cards, drank beer late every night, singing all these crazy songs.

DAVID. That's not right, Dad.

OZZIE. But all that's nothing, I'm sure, to what it must be in war. The things you must touch and see. Honor. You must touch honor. And then one of you is hurt, wounded . . . made blind . . .

DAVID. No. I had fear of all the kinds of dying that there are when I went from here. And then there was this girl with hands and hair like wings. (*The poetry is like a thing possessing him, a frenzy in which he does not know where he is.*) There were candles above the net of gauze under which we lay. Lizards. Cannon could be heard. A girl to weigh no more than dust.

HARRIET. A nurse, right . . . David?

OZZIE. No, no, one of them foreign correspondents, English maybe or French.

Silence.

HARRIET. Oh, how lovely! A Wac or Red Cross girl? . . .

DAVID. No.

OZZIE. Redhead or blonde, Dave?

DAVID. No.

Harriet is shaken.

OZZIE. I mean, what you mean is you whored around a lot. Sure. You whored around. That's what you're saying. You banged some whores . . . had some intercourse. Sure, I mean, that's my point.

(*David, turning away, seems about to rise.*)

Now Dave, take it easy. What I mean is, okay, sure, you shacked up with. I mean, hit on. Hit on, Dave. Dicked. Look at me. I mean, you pronged it, right? Right? Sure, attaboy. (*Patting David on the shoulder*) I mean, it's like going to the bathroom. All glands and secretions. Look, Dave, what are you doing?

(*A rage is building in David, tension forcing him to stand, his cane pressing the floor.*)

We can talk this over. We can talk this over.

(*David, heading for the stairs, crashes into Ozzie.*)

Don't—goddamnit, don't walk away from me. (*He pushes David backward.*) What the hell do you think you're doing? It's what you did. Who the hell you think you are? You screwed it. A yellow whore. Some yellow ass. You put in your prick and humped your ass. You screwed some yellow fucking whore!

(*He has chased David backward, Harriet joining in with him.*)

HARRIET. That's right, that's right. You were lonely and young and away from home for the very first time in your life, no white girls around—

DAVID. They are the color of the earth, and what is white but winter and the earth under it like a suicide?

(Harriet's voice is a high humming in her throat.)

Why didn't you tell me what I was?

(And Harriet vomits, her hands at her mouth, her back turning. There is a silence. They stand. Ozzie starts toward her, falters, starts, reaches, stops.)

OZZIE. Why . . . don't . . . you ask her to cook something for you, David, will you? Make her feel better . . . okay.

DAVID. I think . . . some eggs might be good, Mom.

OZZIE, *wanting to help her.* Hear that, Harriet? David wants some eggs.

HARRIET. I'm *all right.*

OZZIE. Of course you are. *(Patting her tenderly, he offers his clean white handkerchief.)* Here, here: wipe your mouth; you've got a little something—on the corner, left side. That's it. Whattayou say, David?

HARRIET. What's your pleasure, David?

DAVID. Scrambled.

OZZIE. There you go. Your specialty, his pleasure.

(Ozzie, between them, claps his hands; off she goes for the kitchen. Ozzie, looking about the room like a man in deep water looking for something to keep him afloat, sees a pack of cigarettes.)

How about a cigarette? *(Running to grab them, show them)* Filter, see, I switched. Just a little after you left, and I just find them a lot smoother, actually. I wondered if you'd notice. *(And speaking now, his voice and manner take on a confidence; he demonstrates; he is self-assured.)* The filter's granulated. It's an off-product of corn husks. I light up—I feel like I'm on a ship at sea. Isn't that one hell of a good tasting cigarette? Isn't that one beautiful goddamn cigarette?

Harriet enters with two bowls. One has a grapefruit cut in half; the second has eggs and a spoon sticking out.

HARRIET. Here's a little grapefruit to tide you over till I get the eggs.

(And now she stirs the eggs in preparation for scrambling them.)

Won't be long, I promise—but I was just wondering, wouldn't it be nice if we could all go to church tonight. All together and we could make a little visit in thanksgiving of your coming home.

(David is putting his cigarette out in his grapefruit. They see.)

I wouldn't ask that it be long—just—

(He is rising now, dropping the grapefruit on the chair.)

I mean, we could go to whatever saint you wanted, it wouldn't . . . matter . . .

(He has turned his back, is walking toward the stairs.)

Just in . . . just out . . .

(He is climbing the stairs.)

David.

OZZIE. Tired . . . Dave?

(They watch him plodding unfalteringly toward his room.)

Where you going . . . bathroom?

DAVID. No.

OZZIE. Oh.

(David disappears into his room and Harriet whirls and heads for the telephone. Ozzie, startled, turns to look at her.)

Harriet, what's up?

HARRIET. I'm calling Father Donald.

OZZIE. Father Donald?

HARRIET, *dialing.* We need help, I'm calling for help.

OZZIE. Now wait a minute. No; oh, no, we—

HARRIET. Do you still refuse to see it? He was involved with one of them. You know what the Bible says about those people. You heard him.

OZZIE. Just not Father Donald; please, please. That's all I ask—just—

(She is obstinate, he sees. She turns her back waiting for someone to answer.)

Why must everything be personal vengeance?

The front door pops open and in comes bounding Rick, guitar upon his back.

RICK, *happy.* Hi, Mom. Hi, Dad.

HARRIET, *waiting, telephone in hand—overjoyed.* Hi, Rick!

RICK, *happy.* Hi, Mom.

OZZIE, *feeling fine.* Hi, Rick.

RICK. Hi, Dad.

OZZIE. How you doin', Rick? *(He is happy to see good ole regular Rick.)*

RICK. Fine, Dad. You?

OZZIE. Fine.

RICK. Good.

HARRIET. I'll get you some fudge in just a minute, Rick!

RICK. Okay. How's Dave doin', Dad?

He is fiddling with his camera.

OZZIE. Dave's doin' fine, Rick.

RICK. Boy, I'm glad to hear that. I'm really glad to hear that, because, boy, I'll sure be glad when everything's back to the regular way. Dave's too serious, Dad; don't you think so? That's what I think. Whattayou think, Dad?

He snaps a picture of Ozzie, who is posing, smiling, while Harriet waves angrily at them.

HARRIET. SHHHHHHH! *Everybody! (And then, more pleasantly*

she returns to the phone.) Yes, yes. Oh, Father, I didn't recognize your voice. No, I don't know who. Well, yes, it's about my son, Father, David. Yes. Well, I don't know if you know it or not, but he just got back from the war and he's troubled. Deeply. Yes.

(*As she listens silently for a moment, Rick, crouching, snaps a picture of her. She tries to wave him away.*)

Deeply.

(*He moves to another position, another angle, and snaps another picture.*)

Deeply, yes. Oh. So do you think you might be able to stop over some time soon to talk to him or not? Father, any time that would be convenient for you. Yes. Oh, that would be wonderful. Yes. Oh, thank you. And may God reward *you*, Father.

(*Hanging up the phone, she stands a moment, dreaming.*)

OZZIE. I say to myself, what does it mean that he is my son? How the hell is it that . . . he . . . is my son? I mean, they say something of you joined to something of me and became . . . him . . . but what kinda goddamn thing is that? One mystery replacing another? Mystery doesn't explain mystery!

RICK, *scarcely looking up from his comic.* Mom, hey, c'mon, how about that fudge, will ya?

HARRIET. Ricky, oh, I'm sorry. I forgot.

OZZIE. They've got . . . diseases! . . .

HARRIET, *having been stopped by his voice.* What? . . .

OZZIE. Dirty, filthy diseases. They got 'em. Those girls. Infections. From the blood of their parents into the very fluids of their bodies. Malaria, TB. An actual rot alive in them . . . gonorrhea, syphilis. There are some who have the plague. He touched them. It's disgusting. It's—

RICK. Mom, I'm starving, honest to God; and I'm thirsty too.

HARRIET, *as she scurries off, clapping, for the kitchen.* Yes, of course. Oh, oh.

RICK. And bring a piece for Dad, too; Dad looks hungry.

OZZIE. No.

RICK. Sure, a big sweet chocolate piece of fudge.

OZZIE. No. Please. I don't feel well.

RICK. It'll do you good.

HARRIET, *entering with fudge and milk in each hand.* Ricky, here, come here.

RICK, *hurrying toward her.* What?

HARRIET—*hands him fudge and milk.* Look good? (*And she moves toward Ozzie.*)

OZZIE. And something else—maybe it could just be that he's growing away from us, like we did ourselves, only we thought it would happen in some other way, some lesser way.

HARRIET, *putting the fudge and milk into Ozzie's hands.* What are you talking about, "going away"? He's right upstairs.

OZZIE. I don't want that.

HARRIET. You said you did.

OZZIE. He said I did.

RICK, *having gobbled the fudge and milk.* You want me to drive you, Mom?

HARRIET. Would you, Ricky, please?

RICK, *running.* I'll go around and get the car.

HARRIET, *scolding, as Ozzie has put the fudge and milk down on a coffee table.* It's all cut and poured, Ozzie; it'll just be a waste.

OZZIE. I don't care.

HARRIET. You're so childish.

She marches off toward the front door, where she takes a light jacket from a hook, starts to slip it on.

OZZIE. Don't you know I could throw you down onto this floor and make another child live inside you . . . now! . . .

HARRIET. I . . . doubt that . . . Ozzie.

OZZIE. You want me to do it?

HARRIET, *going out the door.* Ohhh, Ozzie, Ozzie.

OZZIE. Sure. Bye-bye. Bye-bye. *(After a pause)* They think they know me and they know nothing. They don't know how I feel. . . . How I'd like to beat Ricky with my fists till his face is ugly! How I'd like to banish David to the streets. . . . How I'd like to cut her tongue from her mouth.

(David moves around upstairs.)

I was myself.

(And now he is clearly speaking to the audience, making them see his value. They are his friends and buddies, and he talks directly to them.)

I lived in a time beyond anything they can ever know—a time beyond and separate, and I was nobody's goddamn father and nobody's goddamn husband! I was myself! And I could run. I got a scrapbook of victories, a bag of medals and ribbons. In the town in which I lived my name was spoken in the factories and in the fields all around because I was the best there was. I'd beaten the finest anybody had to offer. Summer . . . I would sit out on this old wood porch on the front of our house and my strength was in me, quiet and mine. Round the corner would come some old Model T Ford and scampering up the walk this ancient, bone-stiff, buck-toothed farmer, raw as winter and cawing at me like a crow: they had one for me. Out at the edge of town. A runner from another county. My shoes are in a brown-paper bag at my feet. I snatch 'em up. I set out into the dusk, easy as breathing. There's an old white fence and we run for the sun. . . . For a hundred yards or a thousand yards or a thousand thousand. It doesn't matter. Whatever they want. We run the race they think their specialty and I beat them. They sweat and struggle; I simply glide on, one step beyond, no matter what their effort, and the sun bleeds before me. . . . We cross rivers and deserts; we clamber over mountains. I run the races the farmers arrange and win the bets they make. And then a few days after the race, money comes to me anonymously in the mail; but it's not for the money that I run. In the fields and factories they speak my name when they sit down to their lunches. If there's a prize to be run for, it's me they send for. It's to be the-one-sent-for that I run.

David, entering from his room, has listened to the latter part of this.

DAVID. And . . . then . . . you left.

OZZIE, *whirling to look at him.* What?

DAVID. I said . . . "And . . . then you left." That town.

OZZIE. Left?

DAVID. Yes. Went away; traveled.

OZZIE. No. What do you mean?

DAVID. I mean, you're no longer there; you're here . . . now.

OZZIE. But I didn't really *leave* it. I mean, not *leave*. Not really.

DAVID. Of course you did. Where are you?

OZZIE. That's not the point, Dave. Where I am isn't the point at all.

DAVID. But it is. It's everything; all that other is gone. Where are you going?

OZZIE. Groceries. Gotta go get groceries. You want anything at the grocery store? (*He looks at his watch.*) It's late. I gotta get busy.

DAVID, *as Ozzie exits.* That's all right, Dad. That's fine.

Blackout.

The lights rise to brightness, and Rick enters from the kitchen, carrying his guitar, plinking a note or two as Harriet emerges also from the kitchen, carrying a bowl of chips and a tray of drinks, and Ozzie appears upstairs, coming down the hall carrying an 8-mm movie projector already loaded with film.

HARRIET. Tune her up now, Rick.

OZZIE. What's the movie about anyway?

HARRIET. It's probably scenery, don't you think?—trees and fields and those little ponds. Everything over there's so green and lovely. Enough chips, Ricky?

All during this, they scurry about with their many preparations.

RICK. We gonna have pretzels too? 'Cause if there's both pretzels and chips then there's enough chips.

OZZIE, *at the projector.* David shoot it or somebody else? . . . Anybody know? I tried to peek—put a couple feet up to the light . . .

HARRIET. What did you see?

OZZIE. Nothing. Couldn't.

HARRIET. Well, I'll just bet there's one of those lovely little ponds in it somewhere.

OZZIE. Harriet . . . you know when David was talking about that trouble in Hank's hand being congenital, what did you think? You think it's possible? I don't myself. I mean, we knew Hank well. I think it's just something David got mixed up about and nobody corrected him. What do you think? Is that what you think? Whatsamatter? Oh.

He stops, startled, as he sees she is waving at him. Looking up the stairs, which are behind him, he sees David is there, preparing to descend. David wears his robe and a bright-colored tie.

HARRIET. Hello!

OZZIE. Oh. Hey, oh, let me give you a hand. Yes. Yes. You look good. Good to see you.

(And he is on the move to David to help him down the stairs.)

Yes, sir. I think, all things considered, I think we can figure we're over the hump now and it's all downhill and good from here on in. I mean, we've talked things over, Dave, what do you say? The air's been cleared, that's what I mean—the wounds acknowledged, the healing begun. It's the ones that aren't acknowledged —the ones that aren't talked over—they're the ones that do the deep damage. That's always what happens.

HARRIET, *moving to David.* I've baked a cake, David. Happy, happy being home.

David, on his own, finds his way to a chair and sits.

David, Rick, Ozzie, and Harriet

OZZIE. And we've got pop and ice and chips, and Rick is going to sing some songs.

HARRIET. Maybe we can all sing along if we want.

RICK. Anything special you'd like to hear, Dave?

OZZIE. You just sing what you know, Rick; sing what you care for and you'll do it best.

And he and Harriet settle down upon the couch to listen, all smiles.

RICK. How about "Baby, When I Find You"?

HARRIET. Ohhh, that's such a good one.

RICK. Dave, you just listen to me go! I'm gonna build! *(He plays an excited lead into the song.)* I'm gonna build, build, build.

(And he sings.)

Baby, when I find you,
never gonna stand behind you,
gonna, gonna lead
softly at the start,
gently by the heart,
Sweet . . . Love! . . .

Slipping softly to the sea
you and me both mine
wondrous as a green
growing forest vine. . . .

Baby, when I find you,
never gonna stand behind you,
gonna, gonna lead you
softly at the start,
gently by the heart,
Sweet . . . Love! . . .
Baby, when I find you.

OZZIE, *as both he and Harriet clap and laugh.* Ohhh, great, Rick, great. You burn me up with envy, honest to God.

HARRIET. It was just so wonderful. Oh, thank you so much.

RICK. I just love to do it so much, you know?

OZZIE. Has he got something goin' for him, Dave? Huh? Hey! You don't even have a drink. Take this one; take mine!

Now they hurry back and forth from David to the table.

HARRIET. And here's some cake.

OZZIE. How 'bout some pretzels, Dave?

RICK. Tell me what you'd like to hear.

DAVID. I'd like to sing.

This stops them. They stare at David for a beat of silence.

RICK. What?

OZZIE. What's that?

DAVID. I have something I'd like to sing.

RICK. Dave, you don't sing.

DAVID, *reaching at the air.* I'd like to use the guitar, if I could.

HARRIET. What are you saying?

OZZIE. C'mon, you couldn't carry a tune in a bucket and you know it. Rick's the singer, Rick and your mom.

(Not really listening, thinking that his father has gotten every-thing back to normal, Rick strums and strums the guitar, drifting nearer to David.)

C'mon, let's go, that all we're gonna hear?

DAVID. You're so selfish, Rick. Your hair is black; it glistens. You smile. You sing. People think you are the songs you sing. They never see you. Give me the guitar.

And he clamps his hand closed on the guitar, stopping the music.

RICK. Mom, what's wrong with Dave?

DAVID. Give me.

RICK. Listen, you eat your cake and drink your drink, and if you still wanna, I'll let you.

David stands, straining to take the guitar.

David and Rick

DAVID. Now!

HARRIET. Ozzie, make David behave.

OZZIE. Don't you play too roughly. . . .

DAVID. Ricky! . . .

RICK. I don't think he's playing, Dad.

OZZIE (*as David, following Rick, bumps into a chair*). You watch out what you're doing . . .

David drops his glass on the floor, grabs the guitar.

You got cake all over your fingers, you'll get it all sticky, the strings all sticky— (*Struggling desperately to keep his guitar*) Just tell me what you want to hear, I'll do it for you!

HARRIET. What is it? What's wrong?

DAVID. GIVE ME! (*With great anger*) GIVE ME!

OZZIE. David! . . .

And David wrenches the guitar from Rick's hands, sends Rick sprawling, and loops the strap of the guitar over his shoulder, smiling, smiling.

HARRIET. Ohhhh, no, no, you're ruining everything. What's wrong with you?

OZZIE. I thought we were gonna have a nice party—

DAVID. I'm singing! We are!

OZZIE. No, no, I mean a *nice* party—one where everybody's happy!

DAVID. I'm happy. I'm singing. Don't you see them? Don't you see them?

OZZIE. Pardon, Dave?

HARRIET. What . . . are you saying?

DAVID, *changing, turning.* I have some movies. I thought you . . . knew.

HARRIET. Well . . . we . . . do.

OZZIE. Movies?

DAVID. Yes, I took them.

RICK. I thought you wanted to sing.

OZZIE. I mean, they're what's planned, Dave. That's what's up. The projector's all wound and ready. I don't know what you had to get so angry for.

HARRIET. Let's get everything ready.

OZZIE. Sure, sure. No need for all that yelling.

He moves to set up the projector.

DAVID. I'll narrate.

OZZIE. Fine, sure. What's it about anyway?

HARRIET. Are you in it?

OZZIE. Ricky, plug it in. C'mon, c'mon.

DAVID. It's a kind of story.

RICK. What about my guitar?

DAVID. No.

OZZIE. We oughta have some popcorn, though.

HARRIET. Oh, yes, what a dumb movie house, no popcorn, huh, Rick!

Rick switches off the lights.

OZZIE. Let her rip, Dave.

(Dave turns on the projector; Ozzie is hurrying to a seat.)

Ready when you are, C.B.

HARRIET. Shhhhhhh!

OZZIE, *a little child playing.* Let her rip, C.B. I want a new contract, C.B.

The projector runs for a moment. (Note: In proscenium, a screen should be used if possible, or the film may be allowed to seem projected on the fourth wall; in three-quarter or round the screen may be necessary. If the screen is used, nothing must show upon it but a flickering of green.)

HARRIET. Ohhh, what's the matter? It didn't come out, there's nothing there.

DAVID. Of course there is.

HARRIET. Noooo. . . . It's all funny.

DAVID. Look.

OZZIE. It's underexposed, Dave.

DAVID, *moving nearer.* No. Look.

HARRIET. What?

DAVID. They hang in the trees. They hang by their wrists half-severed by the wire.

OZZIE. Pardon me, Dave?

HARRIET. I'm going to put on the lights.

DAVID. NOOOOOO! LOOK! They hang in the greenish haze afflicted by insects; a woman and a man, middle aged. They do not shout or cry. He is too small. Look—he seems all bone, shame in his eyes; his wife even here come with him, skinny also as a broom and her hair is straight and black, hanging to mask her eyes.

The girl, Zung, drifts into the room.

OZZIE. I don't know what you're doing, David; there's nothing there.

DAVID. LOOK! (*And he points.*) They are all bone and pain, uncontoured and ugly but for the peculiar melon-swelling in her middle which is her pregnancy, which they do not see—look! these soldiers who have found her—as they do not see that she is not dead but only dying until saliva and blood bubble at her lips. Look. . . . Yet . . . she dies. Though a doctor is called in to remove the bullet-shot baby she would have preferred . . . to keep since she was dying and it was dead.

(*And Zung silently, drifting, departs.*)

In fact, as it turned out they would have all been better off left to hang as they had been strung on the wire—he with the back of his head blown off and she, the rifle jammed exactly and deeply up into her, with a bullet fired directly into the child living there. For they ended each buried in a separate place; the husband by chance alone was returned to their village, while the wife was dumped into an alien nearby plot of dirt, while the child, too small a piece of meat, was burned. Put into fire, as the shattered legs and arms cut off of men are burned. There's an oven. It is no ceremony. It is the disposal of garbage! . . .

Harriet gets to her feet, marches to the projector, pulls the plug, begins a little lecture.

HARRIET. It's so awful the things those yellow people do to one another. Yellow people hanging yellow people. Isn't that right? Ozzie, I told you—animals—Christ, burn them. David, don't let it hurt you. All the things you saw. People aren't themselves in war. I mean like that sticking that gun into that poor woman and then shooting that poor little baby, that's not human. That's inhuman. It's inhuman, barbaric and uncivilized and inhuman.

DAVID. I'm thirsty.

HARRIET. For what? Tell me. Water? Or would you like some milk? How about some milk?

DAVID, *shaking his head.* No.

HARRIET. Or would you like some orange juice? All golden and little bits of ice.

OZZIE. Just all those words and that film with no picture and these poor people hanging somewhere—so you can bring them home like this house is a meat house—

HARRIET. Oh, Ozzie, no, it's not that—no—he's just young, a young boy . . . and he's been through terrible, terrible things and now he's home, with his family he loves, just trying to speak to those he loves—just—

DAVID. Yes! That's right. Yes. What I mean is, yes, of course, that's what I am—a young . . . blind man in a room . . . in a house in the dark, raising nothing in a gesture of no meaning toward two voices who are not speaking . . . of a certain . . . incredible . . . *connection!*

All stare. Rick leaps up, running for the stairs.

RICK. Listen, everybody, I hate to rush off like this, but I gotta. Night.

HARRIET. Good night, Rick.

OZZIE, *simultaneously.* Good night.

David moves toward the stairs, looking upward.

DAVID. Because I talk of certain things . . . don't think I did them. Murderers don't even know that murder happens.

HARRIET. What are you saying? No, no. We're a family, that's all— we've had a little trouble—David, you've got to stop—please— no more yelling. Just be happy and home like all the others— why can't you?

DAVID. You mean take some old man to a ditch of water, shove his head under, talk of cars and money till his feeble pawing stops, and then head on home to go in and out of doors and drive cars and sing sometimes. I left her like you wanted . . . where people are thin and small all their lives. *(The beginning of realization)* Or did . . . you . . . think it was a . . . place . . . like this? Sinks and kitchens all the world over? Is that what you believe? Water from faucets, light from wires? Trucks, telephones, TV. Ricky sings and sings, but if I were to cut his throat, he would no longer and you would miss him—you would miss his singing. We are hoboes! *(And it is the first time in his life he has ever thought these things.)* We make signs in the dark. You know yours. I understand my own. We share . . . coffee!

(There is nearly joy in this discovery: a hint of new freedom that might be liberation. And somewhere in the thrill of it he has whirled, his cane has come near to Ozzie, frightening him, though Harriet does not notice. Now David turns, moving for the stairs, thinking.)

I'm going up to bed . . . now. . . . I'm very . . . tired.

OZZIE. Well . . . you have a good sleep, Son. . . .

DAVID. Yes, I think I'll sleep in.

OZZIE. You do as you please. . . .

DAVID. Good night.

HARRIET. Good night.

OZZIE. Good night.

HARRIET. Good night. *(Slight pause.)* You get a good rest. *(Silence.)* Try . . .

(Silence. David has gone into his room. Ozzie and Harriet stand.)

I'm . . . hungry . . . Ozzie. . . . Are you hungry?

OZZIE. Hungry? . . .

HARRIET. Yes.

OZZIE. No. Oh, no.

HARRIET. How do you feel? You look a little peaked. Do you feel all right?

OZZIE. I'm fine; I'm fine.

HARRIET. You look funny.

OZZIE. Really. No. How about yourself?

HARRIET. I'm never sick; you know that. Just a little sleepy.

OZZIE. Well . . . that's no wonder. It's been a long day.

HARRIET. Yes, it has.

OZZIE. No wonder.

HARRIET. Good night.

(She is climbing the stairs toward bed.)

OZZIE. Good night.

HARRIET. Don't stay up too late now.

OZZIE. Do you know when he pointed that cane at me, I couldn't breathe. I felt . . . for an instant I . . . might never breathe. . . .

HARRIET. Ohhh . . . I'm so sleepy. So . . . sooooo sleepy. Aren't you sleepy?

OZZIE, *to make her answer.* Harriet! I couldn't breathe.

HARRIET. WHAT DO YOU WANT? TEACHING HIM SPORTS AND FIGHTING.

(This moment—one of almost a primal rage—should be the very first shattering of her motherly self-sacrificing image.)

WHAT . . . OZZIE . . . DO YOU WANT?

OZZIE. Well . . . I was . . . wondering, do we have any aspirin down here . . . or are they all upstairs?

HARRIET. I thought you said you felt well.

OZZIE. Well, I do, I do. It's just a tiny headache. Hardly worth mentioning.

HARRIET. There's aspirin in the desk.

OZZIE, *crossing.* Fine. Big drawer?

HARRIET. Second drawer, right-hand side.

OZZIE. Get me a glass of water, would you, please?

HARRIET. Of course.

She gets a glass from a nearby table, a drink left over from the party, and hands it to him.

OZZIE. Thank you. It's not much of a headache, actually. Actually it's just a tiny headache.

He pops the tablets into his mouth and drinks to wash them down.

HARRIET. Aspirin makes your stomach bleed.

(He tries to keep from swallowing the aspirin, but it is too late.)

Did you know that? Nobody knows why. It's part of how it works. It just does it, makes you bleed. This extremely tiny series of hemorrhages in those delicate inner tissues.

(He is staring at her: there is vengeance in what she is doing.)

It's like those thin membranes begin, in a very minor way, to sweat blood and you bleed; inside yourself you bleed.

She crosses away.

OZZIE. That's not true. None of that. You made all that up. . . . Where are you going?

(With a raincoat on, she is moving out the front door.)

I mean . . . are you going out? Where . . . are you off to?

(She is gone.)

Goddamnit, there's something going on around here, don't you want to know what it is? (*Yelling at the shut door*) I want to know what it is. (*Turning, marching to the phone, dialing*) I want to know what's going on around here. I want to; I do. Want to—got to. Police. That's right, goddamnit—I want one of you people to get on out to seven-seventeen Dunbar and do some checking, some checking at seven-seventeen— What? Ohhh— (*Hissing*) Christ! . . . (*And he is pulling a handkerchief from his pocket, and covering the mouthpiece.*) I mean, they got a kid living there who just got back from the war and something's going on and I want to know what it. . . . No, I don't wanna give my name—it's them, not me— Hey! Hey!

RICK, *popping in at the hallway at the top of the stairs.* Hey, Dad! How you doin'?

Ozzie slams down the phone.

OZZIE. Oh, Rick! Hi!

RICK. Hi! How you doin'?

Guitar over his shoulder, he is heading down the stairs and toward the front door.

OZZIE. Fine. Just fine.

RICK. Good.

OZZIE. How you doin', Rick?

RICK. Well, I'll see you later.

OZZIE, *running.* I WANT YOU TO TEACH ME GUITAR!

RICK, *faltering.* What?

OZZIE. I want you to teach me . . . guitar! . . . To play it.

RICK (*as Ozzie pulls the guitar from his hands*). Sure. Okay.

OZZIE. I want to learn to play it. They've always been a kind of mystery to me, pianos, guitars.

RICK. Mystery?

And Ozzie is trying, awkwardly, desperately, to play.

OZZIE. I mean, what do you think? Do you ever have to think what your fingers should be doing? What I mean is do you ever have to say—I don't know what—"This finger goes there and this other one does—" I mean, "It's on *this* ridge; now I chord all the strings and then switch it all." See? And do you have to tell yourself, "Now switch it all—first finger this ridge—second finger, down—third—somewhere." I mean, does that kind of thing ever happen? I mean, *How do you play it?* I keep having this notion of wanting some . . . thing . . . some material thing, and I've built it. And then there's this feeling I'm of value, that I'm on my way—I mean, moving—and I'm going to come to something eventually, some kind of achievement. All these feelings of a child . . . in me. . . . They shoot through me and then they're gone and they're not anything . . . anymore. But it's . . . a . . . wall . . . that I want . . . I think. I see myself doing it sometimes . . . all brick and stone . . . coils of steel. And then I finish . . . and the success of it is monumental and people come from far . . . to see . . . to look. They applaud. Ricky . . . teach me . . .

RICK. Ahhh . . . what, Dad?

OZZIE. Guitar, guitar.

RICK. Oh, sure. First you start with the basic C chord. You put the first finger on the second string—

OZZIE. But that's what I'm talking about. You don't do that. I know you don't.

RICK, *not understanding.* Oh.

OZZIE. You just pick it up and play it. I don't have time for all that you're saying. That's what I've been telling you.

RICK, *on his way for the door.* Well, maybe some other day then. Maybe Mom'll wanna learn, too.

All this dialogue is rapid, overlapping.

OZZIE. No, no.

RICK. Just me and you then.

OZZIE. Right. Me and you.

RICK. I'll see you later.

OZZIE. What?

RICK. Maybe tomorrow.

OZZIE. No.

RICK. Well, maybe the next day then.

And he is gone out the door.

OZZIE. NOW! Now!

(And the door slams shut.)

I grew too old too quick. I had no choice. It was just a town, I thought, and no one remained to test me. I didn't even know it was leaving I was doing. I thought I'd go away and come back. Not leave. *(And he looks up at David's room.)* YOU SONOFA-BITCH *(running up to David's room)*, NOT LEAVE! *(He bursts into the room. Silence.)* Restless, Dave; restless. Got a lot on my mind. Some of us can't just lay around, you know. You said I left that town like I was wrong, but I was right. A man proved himself out there, tested himself. So I went and then I ended up in the goddamn Depression, what about that? I stood in goddamn lines of people begging bread and soup. You're not the only one who's had troubles. All of us, by God, David; think about that a little. *(Stepping out the door, slamming it)* Just give somebody besides yourself some goddamn thought for a change.

(Pause. He talks to the audience again; they are his friends.)

Lived in goddamn dirty fields, made tents of our coats. The whole length of this country again and again, soot in our fingers, riding the rails, a bum, a hobo, but young. I remember. And then one day . . . on one of those trains, Hank was there, the first time I ever saw him. Hank, the brakeman, and he sees me hunched down in that car and he orders me off. He stands distant, ordering that I jump! . . . I don't understand and then he stops speaking . . . and . . . when he speaks again, pain is in his eyes and voice—"You're a runner," he says. "Christ, I didn't know you were a runner." And he moves to embrace me and with both hands lifts me high above his head—holds me there trembling, then flings me far out and I fall, I roll. All in the air, then slam down breathless, raw from the cinders . . . bruised and dizzy at the outskirts of this town, and I'm here, gone from that other town. I'm here. We become friends, Hank and me, have good times even though things are rough. He likes to point young girls out on the street and tell me how good it feels to touch them. I start thinking of their bodies, having dreams of horses, breasts and crotches. I remember. And then one day the feeling is in me that I must see a train go by and I'll get on it or I won't, something will happen, but halfway down to where I was thrown off, I see how the grass in among the ties is tall, the rails rusted. . . . Grass grows in abundance. No trains any longer come that way; they all go some other way . . . and far behind me Hank is calling, and I turn to see him coming, Harriet young and lovely in his hand, weaving among the weeds. I feel the wonder of her body moving toward me. She's the thing I think I'll enter to find my future. "Hank," I yell, "you sonofabitch! Bring her here. C'mon. Bring her on." Swollen with pride, screaming and yelling, I stand there, I stand: "I'm ready. I'm ready . . . I'm ready."

He has come down the stairs. He stands, arms spread, yelling. Blackout. Music.

Lights slowly up. Ozzie sleeps on the couch. Rick sits in a chair, looking at his guitar. Zung is in David's room, sitting on the bed behind David, who is slouched in a chair. Harriet, dressed in a blue robe, enters from the upstairs hallway and comes down the stairs.

HARRIET. Have you seen my crossword-puzzle book?

RICK. In the bathroom, Mom.

HARRIET. Bathroom? . . . Did I leave it there?

Turning, she heads back up the stairs.

RICK. Guess so, Mom.

DAVID, *sitting abruptly up in his chair as if at a sudden, frightening sound.* Who's there? There's someone there?

(Rick looks up; David is standing, poking the air with his cane.) Who's there?

He opens the door to his room and steps into the hallway.

RICK. Whatsamatter? It's just me and Dad, and Dad's sleeping.

DAVID. Sleeping? Is he?

RICK. On the davenport. . . . You want me to wake him?

DAVID. Nooo . . . nooo.

He moves swiftly to descend to the living room.

RICK. Hey . . . could I get some pictures, Dave? Would you mind?

DAVID. Of course not. No.

RICK, *dashing off up the stairs, while David gropes to find the couch.* Let me just go get some film and some flashes, okay.

DAVID, *standing behind the couch on which Ozzie sleeps and looking after Rick.* Sure . . .

OZZIE. Pardon? Par . . . don?

DAVID, *whispering into his father's ear.* I think you should know I've begun to hate you. I feel the wound of you, yet I don't think you can tell me any more, I . . . must tell you. If I had been an orphan with no one to count on me, I would have stayed there. Now . . . she is everywhere I look. I can see nothing to distract me.

(Ozzie stirs.)

You think us good, we steal all you have.

OZZIE. Good . . . ole Hank. . . .

DAVID. No, no, he has hated us always—always sick with rot.

OZZIE. Noooo . . . nooooooo. . . .

DAVID. She would tell me you would not like her. She would touch her fingers to her eyes, and she knew how I must feel sometimes as you do.

OZZIE. Ohhh, noooo . . . sleeping. . . .

DAVID. You must hear me. It is only fraud that keeps us sane, I swear it.

OZZIE. David, sleeping! . . . Oh, oh . . .

DAVID. It is not innocence I have lost. What is it I have lost?

OZZIE. Oh . . . oh . . .

Rick has appeared high in the hallway and hesitates there.

DAVID. Don't you know? Do you see her in your sleep?

RICK, *hurrying down.* I meant to get some good shots at the party, but I never got a chance the way things turned out. You can stay right there.

DAVID, *moving toward the chair on which Rick's guitar rests.* I'll sit, all right?

Rick rushes to save the guitar.

RICK. Sure. How you feelin' anyway, Dave? I mean, honest ta God, I'm hopin' you get better. Everybody is. I mean . . . *(He takes a picture.)* . . . you're not gonna go talkin' anymore crazy like about that guitar and all that, are you? You know what I mean. Not to Mom and Dad anyway. It scares 'em and then I get scared and I don't like it, okay?

(He moves on, taking more pictures.)

DAVID. Sure. That guitar business wasn't serious anyway, Rick. None of that. It was all just a little joke I felt like playing, a kind of little game. I was only trying to show you how I hate you.

RICK. Huh? *(Stunned, he stares.)*

DAVID. To see you die is why I live, Rick.

RICK. Oh.

HARRIET, *appearing from off upstairs, the crossword-puzzle book in her hands.* Goodness gracious, Ricky, it was just where you said it would be, though I'm sure I don't know how it got there because I didn't put it there. Hello, David.

DAVID. Hello.

OZZIE. OHHHHHHHHHHHHHHHH! *(Screaming, he comes awake, falling off the couch.)* Oh, boy, what a dream! Oh. . . . *(Trying to get to his feet, but collapsing)* Ohhhhhhh! God, leg's asleep. Jesus! *(And he flops about, sits there rubbing his leg)* Ohhhh, everybody. Scared hell out of me, that dream. I hollered. Did you hear me? And my leg's asleep, too.

(He hits the leg, stomps the floor. Harriet sits on the couch, working her crossword-puzzle book. Rick, slumped in a chair,

reads a comic. David, though, leans forward in his chair. He wants to know the effect of his whispering on his father.)

Did anybody hear me holler?

HARRIET. Not me.

RICK. What did you dream about, Dad?

OZZIE. I don't remember, but it was awful. *(Stomping the foot)* Ohhhh, wake up, wake up. Hank was in it, though. And Dave. They stood over me, whispering—I could feel how they hated me.

RICK. That really happened; he really did that, Dad.

OZZIE. Who did?

RICK. What you said.

OZZIE. No. No, I was sleeping. It scared me awful in my sleep. I'm still scared, honest ta God, it was so awful.

DAVID. It's that sleeping in funny positions, Dad. It's that sleeping in some place that's not a bed.

OZZIE. Pardon?

DAVID. Makes you dream funny. What did Hank look like?

HARRIET. Ozzie, how do you spell "Apollo"?

OZZIE. What?

RICK. Jesus, Dad, Schroeder got three home runs, you hear about that? Two in the second of the first and one in the third of the second. Goddamn, if he don't make MVP in the National, I'll eat my socks. You hear about that, Dad?

OZZIE. Yes, I did. Yes.

RICK. He's somethin'.

OZZIE. A pro.

HARRIET. Ozzie, can you think of a four letter word that starts with G and ends with B?

RICK. Glub.

HARRIET. Glub?

OZZIE *(almost simultaneously).* Glub?

RICK. It's a cartoon word. Cartoon people say it when they're drowning. G-L-U-B.

OZZIE, *on his feet now.* Ricky. Ricky, I was wondering . . . when I was sleeping, were my eyes open? Was I seeing?

RICK. I didn't notice, Dad.

HARRIET. *Glub* doesn't work, Rick.

RICK. Try *grub.* That's what sourdoughs call their food. It's G-R—

OZZIE. WAIT A MINUTE!

RICK. G-R—

OZZIE. ALL OF YOU WAIT A MINUTE! LISTEN! Listen. I mean, I look for explanations. I look inside myself. For an explanation. I mean, I look inside *my* self. As I would look into water . . . or the sky . . . the ocean. They're silver. Answers . . . silver and elusive . . . like fish. But if you can catch them in the sea . . . hook them as they flash by, snatch them . . . drag them down like birds from the sky . . . against all their struggle . . . when you're adrift . . . and starving . . . they . . . can help you live.

He falters; he stands among them, straining to go further, searching some sign of comprehension in their faces.

RICK. Mom . . . Dad's hungry . . . I think. He wants some fish, I—

OZZIE. SHUT UP!

RICK, *hurt deeply.* Dad?

OZZIE. PIECE OF SHIT! SHUT UP! SHUT UP!

HARRIET. Ozzie! . . .

OZZIE, *roaring down at David.* I don't want to hear about her. I'm not interested in her. You did what you did and I was no part of it. You understand me? I don't want to hear any more about her! Look at him. Sitting there. Listening. I'm tired of hearing you, Dave. You understand that? I'm tired of hearing you and your crybaby voice and your crybaby stories. And your crybaby slobbering and your . . . (And his voice is possessed with astonished loathing.) LOOK . . . AT . . . HIM! YOU MAKE ME WANT TO VOMIT! HARRIET! YOU— (He whirls on Harriet.) YOU! Your internal organs—your internal female organs—they've got some kind of poison in them. They're backing up some kind of rot into the world. I think you ought to have them cut out of you. I MEAN, I JUST CAN'T STOP THINKING ABOUT IT. I JUST CAN'T STOP THINKING ABOUT IT. LITTLE BITTY CHINKY KIDS HE WANTED TO HAVE! LITTLE BITTY CHINKY YELLOW KIDS! DIDN'T YOU! FOR OUR GRANDCHILDREN! (And he slaps David with one hand.) LITTLE BITTY YELLOW PUFFY— (He breaks, groping for the word.) . . . creatures! . . . FOR OUR GRAND-CHILDREN! (He slaps David again, again.) THAT'S ALL YOU CARED!

David, a howl in his throat, has stood up.

HARRIET. Ohhh, Ozzie, God forgive you the cruelty of your words. All children are God's children.

David is standing rigid. The front door blows open, and in a fierce and sudden light Zung steps forward to the edge of David's room, as he looks up at her.

DAVID. I didn't know you were here. I didn't know. I will buy you clothing. I have lived with them all my life. I will make them not hate you. I will buy you boots.

(And he is moving toward her, climbing the stairs.)

They will see you. The seasons will amaze you. Texas is enormous. Ohio is sometimes green. There will be time. We will learn to speak. And it will be as it was in that moment when we looked in the dark and our eyes were tongues that could speak and the hurting . . . all of it . . . stopped, and there was total understanding in you of me and in me of you . . . and . . .

(Near her now, stepping into his room through the wall, he reaches in a tentaive way toward her.)

such delight in your eyes that I felt it;

Zung and David

(And she has begun to move away from him.)

yet . . . I

(She is moving away and down the stairs.)

discarded you. I discarded you. Forgive me. You moved to leave as if you were struggling not to move, not to leave. "She's the thing most possibly of value in my life," I said. "She is garbage and filth and I must get her back if I wish to live. Sickness. I must cherish her." Zung, there were old voices inside me I had trusted all my life as if they were my own. I didn't know I shouldn't hear them. So reasonable and calm they seemed a source of wisdom. "She's all of everything impossible made possible, cast her down," they said. "Go home." And I did as they told; and now I know that I am not awake but asleep, and in my sleep . . . there is nothing. . . .

(Zung is now standing before the open door, facing it, about to leave.)

Nothing! . . . What do you want from me to make you stay? I'll do it. I'll do what you want!

RICK, *in the dark before his father, camera in hand.* Lookee here, Dad. Cheer up! Cheer up!

DAVID *(as Zung turns to look up at him).* Nooooooooo. . . .

(And there is a flash as Rick takes the picture.)

NOOOOOOOOOOOOOOO! STAAAAAAAY!

And the door slams shut, leaving Zung still inside. A slide of Ozzie appears on the screen, a close-up of his pained and puzzled face. Music, a falling of notes. The lights are going to black. Perhaps "Intermission" is on the bottom of the slide. The slide blinks out.

ACT TWO

Blackness. Slide: color close-up of a man's ruddy, smiling, round face.

1ST CHILD'S VOICE. Who zat?

WOMAN'S VOICE. I don't know.

MAN'S VOICE. Looks like a neighbor.

WOMAN'S VOICE. How can you say it's a neighbor? You don't know.

New slide appears: scenery, in color.

2ND CHILD'S VOICE. Oh, that's a pretty one.

New slide: Father Donald in a boxing pose, color.

1ST CHILD'S VOICE. Oh, lookee that.

MAN'S VOICE. Father What's-his-name. You know.

Another slide: Father Donald, slightly different boxing pose.

WOMAN'S VOICE. There he is again.

2ND CHILD'S VOICE. Wow.

Lights up on the downstairs. David is up in his room on his bed. Downstairs, Harriet sits on the couch, Father Donald is on a chair; Ozzie is in the chair beside him. We have the feeling they have been there a long, long time.

FATHER DONALD. I deal with people and their uneasiness on a regular basis all the time, you see. Everybody I talk to is nervous . . . one way or another . . . so . . . I anticipate no real trouble in dealing with Dave. You have no idea the things people do and then tell me once that confessional door is shut. I'm looking forward actually, to speaking with him. Religion has been sloughed off a lot lately, but I think there's a relevancy much larger than the credit most give. We're growing—and our insights, when we have them, are twofold. I for one have come recently to understand how very often what seems a spiritual problem is in fact a problem of the mind rather than the spirit—not that the two can in fact be separated, though, in theory, they very often are. So what we must do is apply these theories to fact. At which point we would find that mind and spirit are one and I, a priest, am a psychiatrist, and psychiatrists are priests. I mean— I feel like I'm rambling. Am I rambling?

HARRIET. Oh, no, Father.

OZZIE. Nooo . . . noo.

HARRIET. Father, this is hard for me to say, but I . . . feel . . . his problem is he sinned against the sixth commandment with whores.

FATHER DONALD. That's very likely over there.

HARRIET. And then the threat of death each day made it so much worse.

FATHER DONALD. I got the impression from our earlier talk that he'd had a relationship of some duration.

HARRIET. A day or two, wouldn't you say, Ozzie?

OZZIE, *distracted, oddly preoccupied with his chair.* A three-day pass I'd say . . . though I don't know, of course.

FATHER DONALD. They're doing a lot of psychiatric studies on that phenomenon right now, did you know that?

The front door pops open, and in bounds Rick.

HARRIET. Oh, Rick! . . .

RICK. Hi, Mom. Hi, Dad.

OZZIE. Hi, Rick.

FATHER DONALD, *rising.* Rick, hello!

RICK. Oh, Father Donald . . . hi.

No time for Father Donald, Rick is speeding for the kitchen.

OZZIE. Look at him heading for the fudge.

FATHER DONALD. Well, he's a good big strong sturdy boy.

RICK, *as he goes out.* Hungry and thirsty.

FATHER DONALD. And don't you ever feel bad about it, either!

(He stands for an instant, a little uncertain what to do.)

Dave's up in his room, I imagine, so maybe I'll just head on up and have my little chat. He is why I'm here, after all.

HARRIET. Fine.

OZZIE, *standing, still distracted, he stares at the chair in which Father Donald was sitting.* First door top of the stairs.

FATHER DONALD. And could I use the bathroom, please, before I see ole Dave? Got to see a man about a horse.

HARRIET. Oh, Father, certainly: it's just down the hall. Fifth door.

OZZIE, *stepping nearer to the chair.* What's wrong with that chair? . . .

HARRIET. It's the blue door, Father! . . .

OZZIE. I . . . don't like that chair. I think it's stupid . . . looking. . . .

(As Rick enters from the kitchen, eating fudge)

Ricky, sit. Sit in that chair.

RICK. What? . . .

OZZIE. Go on, sit, sit.

Rick hurries to the chair, sits, eats. Ozzie is fixated on the chair.

HARRIET. Oh, Ricky, take your father's picture, he looks so silly.

OZZIE. I just don't think that chair is any good. I just don't think it's comfortable. Father Donald looked ill at ease all the while he was sitting there.

Father Donald, Ozzie, and Harriet

HARRIET. Well, he had to go to the bathroom, Ozzie, what do you expect?

OZZIE, *to Ricky.* Get up. It's just not right.

(Rick gets up and Ozzie flops into the chair, sits, fidgets. Rick goes back out to the kitchen.)

Noooooo. It's just not a comfortable chair at all, I don't know why.

(He rises and moves toward the couch.)

I don't like it. How much did we pay?

HARRIET. What do you think you're doing?

OZZIE. And this couch isn't comfortable either.

HARRIET. It's a lovely couch.

OZZIE—*tests it.* But it isn't comfortable. Noooo. And I'm not really sure it's lovely, either. Did we pay two hundred dollars?

HARRIET. What? Oh, more.

OZZIE. How much?

HARRIET. I don't know, I told you.

OZZIE. You don't. I don't. It's gone anyway, isn't it?

HARRIET. Ozzie, what does it matter?

OZZIE, *already on the move for the stairs.* I'm going upstairs. I'll be upstairs.

HARRIET. Wait a minute.

(As he keeps moving, up the stairs)

I want to talk to you. *I think we ought to talk!*

(Emotion well beneath her voice stops him, turns him.)

I mean, it's nothing to worry about or anything, but you don't know about it and it's your house, you're involved—so it's just something I mention. You're the man of the house, you ought to know. The police were here . . . earlier today.

OZZIE. What? Oh, my God.

HARRIET. The police. Two of them. Two. A big and a small . . . they—

(He is dazed; he doesn't know whether to go up or down, listen or leave. He nods.)

It was just a little bit ago; not long at all.

OZZIE. Jesus Christ. *(He descends.)*

HARRIET. Oh, I know, I know. Just out of the blue like that—it's how I felt, too. I did, I did.

OZZIE. *What—police?*

HARRIET. It was when you were gone for groceries. I mean, they thought they were supposed to be here. We wanted it, they thought.

OZZIE. No, no.

HARRIET. Somebody called them to come here. They thought it had been us. They were supposed to look through David's luggage, they thought.

OZZIE. They . . . were . . . what?

HARRIET. That's what I mean. That's exactly what I—

OZZIE. *Look through his luggage? There's nothing wrong with his luggage!*

HARRIET. Isn't it incredible? Somebody called them—they didn't know who—no name was given and it sounded muffled through a handkerchief, they said. I said, "Well, it wasn't us." Told them, "Don't you worry; we're all all right here." It must have been a little joke by somebody.

OZZIE. What about Dave?

HARRIET. No, no.

OZZIE. Or Ricky? Did you ask Ricky?

HARRIET. Ricky?

OZZIE. RICKY! RICKY!

RICK, *popping in from the kitchen, thinking he was called.* What's up, Dad?

OZZIE. I DON'T KNOW.

RICK. I thought you called.

He pops back out into the kitchen.

OZZIE, *to Harriet.* You ask him; you ask him. I think the whole thing's preposterous—absolutely—

HARRIET, *as Rick re-emerges to look and listen.* Ricky, do you know anything about anybody calling the police to come here?

OZZIE, *turning and moving for the stairs.* I'm going upstairs. I'll be upstairs.

RICK. The police?

(As Harriet turns to look and half step after Ozzie)

Oh, no, Mom, not me. Okay if I use the car?

HARRIET. What?

FATHER DONALD, *encountering Ozzie in the upstairs hallway.* Gonna take care of old Dave right now.

OZZIE. I'm going upstairs. I'll be upstairs.

He exits, as Harriet stands looking up at them.

RICK. Bye, Mom.

HARRIET. What? Oh. (*Looking back as Rick goes out the door*) BE CAREFUL!

FATHER DONALD, *after a slight hesitation.* Ozzie said to tell you he was going upstairs.

HARRIET. What?

FATHER DONALD. Ozzie said to tell you he was going upstairs.

HARRIET—*stares at him a moment.* Oh, Father, I'm so glad you're here.

And she exits into the kitchen, leaving Father Donald. He nods, knocks on David's door.

FATHER DONALD. Dave?

(He opens the door, eases into the semidark of the room.)

Dave? It's me . . . Dave. . . .

(Finding a light, he flicks it on.)

Ohh, Dave, golly, you look just fine. Here I expected to see you all worn out and there you are looking so good. It's me, Dave, Father Donald. Let me shake your hand.

(David's rising hand comes up far off from Father Donald. The priest, his own hand extended, has to move nearly around the bed before he can shake David's hand.)

No, no, David. Here. Over here. Can't see me, can you? There you go. Yes, sir, let me tell you, I'm proud. A lot of people might tell you that, I know, but I mean it, and I'll stand behind it if there's anything I can do for you—anything at all.

DAVID. No. I'm all right.

FATHER DONALD. And that's the amazing part of it, Dave, you are. You truly are. It's plain as day. Golleee, I just don't know how to tell you how glad I am to see you in such high fine spirits. Would you like my blessing? *(He gets to his feet.)* Let me just give you my blessing and then we'll talk things over a little and—

David slashes with his cane and strikes the hand moving into the position to bless.)

Ohhhhhhhhhhhhhhh! *(Wincing, teeth gritted)* Oh, Dave; oh, watch out what you're doing!

DAVID. I know.

FATHER DONALD. No, no, I mean, you swung it in the air, you—hit me.

DAVID. Yes.

FATHER DONALD. No, no, you don't understand, you—

DAVID. I was trying to hit you, Father.

Father Donald stares, taking this in.

FATHER DONALD. What?

DAVID. I didn't send for you.

FATHER DONALD. I know, I know, your poor mother—your poor mother—

DAVID. I don't want you here, Father; get out!

FATHER DONALD. David!

DAVID. Get out, I'm sick of you. You've been in one goddamn corner or another of this room all my life making signs at me, whispering, wanting to splash me with water or mark me with oil—some goddamn hocus-pocus. I feel reverence for the air and the air is empty, Father. Now get the fuck out of here.

FATHER DONALD. No, no, no, no, David. No, no. I can't give that to you. You'll have to get that from somewhere else.

DAVID. I don't want anything from you!

FATHER DONALD. I'm supposed to react now in some foolish way—I see—some foolish, foolish way that will discredit me—isn't that right? Oh, of course it is. It's an excuse to dismiss my voice that you're seeking, an excuse for the self-destruction your anger has made you think you want, and I'm supposed to give it. I'm supposed to find all this you're doing obscene and sacrilegious instead of seeing it as the gesture of true despair that it is. You're trying to make me disappear, but it's not going to happen. No, no. No such luck, David. I understand you, you see. Everything about you.

DAVID. Do you?

FATHER DONALD. The way you're troubled.

DAVID. I didn't know that, Father.

FATHER DONALD. You say that sarcastically—"Do you? I didn't know that." As if to imply you're so complicated I couldn't ever understand you when I already have. You see, I've been looking into a few things, David, giving some things some thought. *(Producing a magazine with a colorful cover)* I have in my hand a magazine—you can't see it, I know—but it's there. A psychiatric journal in which there is an article of some interest and it deals with soldiers and some of them carried on as you did and then there's some others who didn't. It's not all just a matter of hocus-pocus any longer.

DAVID. Carried . . . on . . . Father?

FATHER DONALD. That whore. That yellow whore. You understand.

You knew I was bringing the truth when I came which is why you hit me.

DAVID. I thought you didn't even know the problem. You came in here all bubbly and jolly asking how did I feel.

FATHER DONALD. That was only a little ruse, David; a little maneuver to put you off your guard. I only did that to mislead you. That's right. Your mother gave me all the basics some weeks ago and I filled in the rest from what I know. You see, if it's a fight you want, it's what you'll get. Your soul is worth some time and sweat from me. You're valued by others, David, even if you don't value yourself. (*Waving the magazine in the air*) It's all here—right here—in these pages. It was demonstrated beyond any possible doubt that people—soldiers—who are compelled for some reason not even they themselves understand to establish personal sexual relationships with whores are inferior to those who don't; they're maladjusted, embittered, non-goal-oriented misfits. The sexual acceptance of another person, David, is intimate and extreme; this kind of acceptance of an alien race is in fact the rejection of one's own race—it is in fact the rejection of one's own self—it is sickness, David. Now I'm a religious man, a man of the spirit, but knowledge is knowledge and I must accept what is proven fact whether that fact come from science or philosophy or whatever. What kind of man are you that you think you can deny it? You're in despair, David, whether you think of it that way or not. It's only into a valley of ruin that you are trying to lock yourself. You can only die there, David. Accept me. Let God open your eyes; let Him. He will redeem you. Not I nor anyone, but only Him—yet if you reject me, you reject Him. My hand is His. His blessing.

(*The hand is rising as if the very words elevate it.*)

My blessing. Let me give you my blessing.

(*And David's cane hits like a snake. Father Donald cries out in surprise and pain. He recovers and begs*)

Let me bless you. (*His hand is again rising in blessing.*) Please!

(*David, striking again, stands. He hits again and again.*)

David! David! (*Terrified*) Stop it. Let me bless you.

David hits Father Donald's arm, hits his leg.

DAVID. I don't want you here!

FATHER DONALD. You don't know what you're saying.

(But now the blow seems about to come straight down on his head. He yells and covers his head with his arms. The blow hits. He picks up a chair, holds it up for protection.)

Stop it. Stop it. Goddamnit, stop hitting me. Stop it. You are in despair.

(He slams the chair down.)

A man who hits a priest is in despair!

(Whistling, the cane slams into his arm.)

Ohhhhh, this pain—this terrible pain in my arm—I offer it to earn you your salvation.

DAVID. Get out!

FATHER DONALD. Death! Do you understand that. Death. Death is your choice. You are in despair.

He turns to leave.

DAVID. And may God reward *you*, Father.

FATHER DONALD, *turning back, as David flops down on the bed.* Oh yes; yes of course, you're so confident now, young and strong. Look at you—full of spunk, smiling. But all that'll change. Your tune'll change in time. What about pain, Dave? Physical pain. What do you do when it comes? Now you send me away, but in a little while you'll call me back, run down by time, lying with death on your bed . . . in an empty house . . . gagging on your own spit you cannot swallow; you'll call me then, nothing left to you but fear and Christ's black judging eyes about to find and damn you; you'll call.

Slight pause.

DAVID. That's not impossible, Father.

FATHER DONALD. I don't even like you; do you know that? I DON'T EVEN LIKE YOU!

DAVID. Tell them I hit you when you go down.

FATHER DONALD, *near the door, thinking about trying to bless from there.* No. No, they've pain enough already.

DAVID. Have they? You get the fuck out of here before I kill you.

As if he has read Father Donald's mind and knows what the man is thinking, David's cane has risen like a spear; it aims at the priest's heart.

FATHER DONALD, *moving not a muscle.* THOUGH I DO NOT MOVE MY HAND, I BLESS YOU! YOU ARE BLESSED!

And he exits hurriedly, heading straight down the hall toward the bathroom. Lights up downstairs: it seems a lovely afternoon as Rick and Harriet enter from the kitchen, chatting.

HARRIET. So the thing I want to do—I just think it would be so nice if we could get Dave a date with some nice girl.

RICK. Oh, sure.

HARRIET. Do you think that would be a good idea?

Ozzie, descending from the attic, pauses to peek into David's room; he finds David asleep, and, after a moment, continues on down.

RICK. Sure.

HARRIET. Do you know any girls you think might get along with David?

RICK. No, but I still think it's really a good idea and I'll keep it in mind for all the girls I meet and maybe I'll meet one. Here comes Dad. Hi, Dad. Bye, Mom.

HARRIET. Oh, Ozzie, did you see what they were doing?

OZZIE. Dave's sleeping, Harriet; Father Donald's gone.

HARRIET. What? He can't be gone.

OZZIE. I thought maybe he was down here. How about the kitchen?

HARRIET. No, no, I just came out of the kitchen. Where were you upstairs? Are you sure he wasn't in David's room?

OZZIE. I was in the attic.

HARRIET. Well, maybe he saw the light and came up to join you and you missed each other on the way up and down. Why don't you go check?

OZZIE. I turned off all the lights, Harriet. The attic's dark now.

HARRIET. Well, yell up anyway—

OZZIE. But the attic's dark now, Harriet.

HARRIET. Just in case.

OZZIE. What are you trying to say? Father Donald's up in the attic in the dark? I mean, if he was up there and I turned off the lights, he'd have said something—"Hey, I'm here," or something. It's stupid to think he wouldn't.

And he sits down.

HARRIET. No more stupid to think that than to think he'd leave without telling us what happened with David.

OZZIE. All right, all right. (*Storming to the foot of the stairs*) HEEEEEEYYYYYYYYYYYYY! HEEEEYYYYYYYY! UP THEEEEERRE! ANYBODY UP THERE?

There is a brief silence. He turns toward Harriet.

DAVID, *on his bed in his room.* WHAT'S THAT, DAD?

OZZIE—*falters, looks about.* What?

DAVID. WHAT'S UP, DAD?

OZZIE. OH, DAVE, NO, NOT YOU.

DAVID. WHY ARE YOU YELLING?

OZZIE. NO, NO, WE JUST THOUGHT FATHER DONALD WAS UP THERE IN THE ATTIC, DAVE. DON'T YOU WORRY ABOUT IT.

DAVID. I'M THE ONLY ONE UP HERE, DAD!

OZZIE. BUT . . . YOU'RE NOT IN THE ATTIC, SEE?

DAVID. I'M IN MY ROOM.

OZZIE. I KNOW YOU'RE IN YOUR ROOM.

DAVID. YOU WANT ME TO GO UP IN THE ATTIC?

OZZIE. NO! GODDAMNIT, JUST—

DAVID. I DON'T KNOW WHAT YOU WANT.

OZZIE. I WANT YOU TO SHUT UP, DAVE, THAT'S WHAT I WANT, JUST—

FATHER DONALD, *appearing from off upstairs.* What's the matter? What's all the yelling?

HARRIET. Oh, Father!

OZZIE. Father, hello, hello.

HARRIET. How did it go? Did it go all right?

FATHER DONALD, *coming down the steps, seeming as if nothing out of the ordinary has happened.* Fine, just fine.

HARRIET. Oh, you're perspiring so though—look at you.

FATHER DONALD, *maneuvering for the door.* Well, I've got a lot on my mind. It happens. Nerves. I've other appointments. Many, many.

HARRIET. You mean you're leaving? What are you saying?

FATHER DONALD. I must.

HARRIET. But we've got to talk.

FATHER DONALD. Call me.

HARRIET. Father . . . bless me! . . .

FATHER DONALD. What? . . .

HARRIET. Bless me. . . .

FATHER DONALD. Of course.

She bows her head, and the priest blesses her, murmuring the Latin.

HARRIET. Ohhh, Father, thank you so much. (*Touching his hand*) Shall I walk you to your car?

FATHER DONALD, *backing for the door.* Fine, fine. That's all right. Sure.

OZZIE, *nodding.* DAVE, SAY GOOD-BYE TO FATHER DONALD, HE'S LEAVING NOW.

FATHER DONALD. GOOD-BYE, DAVE!

DAVID. GOOD-BYE, FATHER!

Blackout as Harriet and Father Donald are going out the door. Music.

Ozzie is discovered in late night light, climbing the stairs to David's door, where, after hesitating an instant, he gently knocks.

OZZIE. Dave, I'd like to come in . . . if I could. *(Easing in)* Awful dark; can I put on a light?

(Silence.)

I mean, we don't need one—not really. I just thought we might . . . I mean, first of all, I want to apologize for the way I hit you the other day. I don't know why I did it. I'm . . . gonna sit down here on the edge of the bed. Are you awake enough to understand? I am your father, you know, and I could command . . . if I wanted. I don't; but I could. I'm going to sit.

(Slight pause.)

I mean, it's so sad the way you just go on and on . . . and I'd like to have time for you, but you want so much; I have important things, too. I have plans; I'm older, you know; if I fail to fulfill them, who will do it: Not you, though you could. And Rick's too busy. Do you understand? There's no evidence in the world of me, no sign or trace, as if everything I've ever done were no more than smoke. My life has closed behind me like water. But I must not care about it. I must not. Though I have inside me a kind of grandeur I can't realize, many things and memories of a darker time when we were very different—harder—nearer to the air and we thought of nothing as a gift. But I can't make you see that. There's no way. It's what I am, but it's not what you are. Even if I had the guitar, I would only stand here telling my fingers what to do, but they would do nothing. You would not see. . . . I can't get beyond these hands. I jam in the fingers. I break on the bone. I am . . . lonely. I mean, oh, no, not exactly lonely, not really. That's a little strong, actually. . . .

(Silence.)

I mean . . . Dave . . . *(He pulls from his back pocket David's overseas cap.)* What's this?

DAVID. What?

OZZIE. This cap. What is it? I cut myself on it. I was rummaging in your stuff upstairs, your bags and stuff, and I grabbed it. It cut me.

DAVID, *reaching for the cap.* Oh . . . yes.

OZZIE. There are razors sewn into it. Why is that?

DAVID. To cut people.

Slowly he puts the cap on his head.

OZZIE. Oh.

DAVID. Here . . . I'll show you. . . . *(Getting slowly to his feet)* You're on the street, see. You walk . . . and see someone who's after you. . . . You wait. . . .

(He tenses. His hand rises to the tip of the cap.)

As they get near . . . slowly you remove the hat—they think you're going to toss it aside, see? You . . . *snap it! You snap it!*

(Seizing the front edge of the cap between thumb and finger, he snaps it down. It whistles past Ozzie, who jumps.)

It cuts them. They hold their face. However you want them, they're yours. You can stomp them, kick them. This is on the street. I'd like to do that to somebody, wouldn't you?

OZZIE. Huh?

DAVID. It'd be fun.

OZZIE. Oh, sure. I . . .

DAVID. Hank told you to buy this house, didn't he?

OZZIE. What?

DAVID. "Get that house," he said. "Get it."

OZZIE. It's a good house. Solid. Not one of those prefabs, those—

DAVID. It's a coffin. You made it big so you wouldn't know, but that's what it is, and not all the curtains and pictures and lamps in the world can change it. He threw you off a fast free train, Ozzie.

OZZIE. I don't believe you saw him.

DAVID. He told you gold, he gave you shit.

OZZIE. I don't believe you saw him. You're a liar, David.

Zung appears.

DAVID. Do you know, Dad, it seemed sometimes I would rise and slam with my fists into the walls of a city. Pointing at buildings, I turned them into fire. I took the fleeing people into my fingers and bent them to touch their heads to their heels, each scream-ing at the sight of their brain turning black. And now sometimes I miss them, all those screaming people. I wish they were here with us, you and Mom and Rick and Zung and me.

Pause.

OZZIE. Mom and Rick and who and you, Dave?

DAVID. Zung.

Zung is moving nearer to them now.

OZZIE. Zung, Dave?

DAVID. She's here. They were all just hunks of meat that had no mind to know of me until I cared for her. It was simple. We lived in a house. She didn't want to come back here, Dad; she wanted me to stay there. And in all the time I knew her, she cost me six dollars that I had to sneak into her purse. Surprised? In time I'll show you some things. You'll see them. I will be your fa-ther.

He tosses the cap at Ozzie.

OZZIE, *shaken, struggling to catch the cap.* Pardon, Dave?

DAVID. What's wrong? You sound like something's terribly wrong?

OZZIE. No. No, no. I'm fine. Your poor mother—she's why I'm here. Your poor mother, sick with grief. She's mine to care for, you know. It's me you're after, yet you torment her. No more. No more. That's what I came up here to tell you.

DAVID, *getting to his feet.* Good.

OZZIE. You're phony, David—phony—trying to make up for the thousands you butchered, when if you were capable of love at all you would love us, your mother and me—not that we matter—instead of some poor little whore who isn't even here.

DAVID, *exiting the room.* I know.

OZZIE. I want her happy.

DAVID (*as Ozzie follows a little into the hall*). I know.

And David is gone. Harriet enters slowly from the kitchen, sees Ozzie, then the room's open door.

HARRIET. Did you have a nice talk?

OZZIE, *heading toward her.* Harriet, what would you say if I said I wanted some checking done?

HARRIET. I don't know what you mean. In what way do you mean?

OZZIE. Take a look at that. But just be careful.

HARRIET. What is it?

OZZIE. His cap. There are razor blades sewn in it; all along the edge.

HARRIET. Ozzie . . . ohhh! Goodness.

OZZIE. That's what I mean. And I was reading just yesterday—some of them bring back guns and knives. Bombs. We've got somebody living in this house who's killed people, Harriet, and that's a fact we've got to face. I mean, I think we ought to do some checking. You know that test where they check teeth against old X-rays. I think—

HARRIET. Ohhh . . . my God! . . .

OZZIE. I know, I know, it scares me, too, but what are we talking about? We're talking about bombs and guns and knives, and sometimes I don't even think it's David up there. I feel funny . . . sometimes . . . I mean, and I want his fingerprints taken. I think we should have his blood type—

HARRIET. Oh, Ozzie, Ozzie, it was you.

OZZIE. Huh?

HARRIET. You did it. You got this out of his luggage, all his baggage upstairs. You broke in and searched and called the police.

OZZIE. No. What?

HARRIET. You told them to come here, and then you lied and said you didn't.

OZZIE. What?

HARRIET. You did, and then you lied and now you're lying again.

OZZIE. Oh, no. No.

HARRIET. What's wrong with you? What's happening to you?

OZZIE. But I didn't do that. I didn't.

(David appears in the upstairs hallway, moving to return to his room.)

I didn't. No, no. And even if I did, what would it mean but I changed my mind, that's all. Sure. *(Looking up at David moving in the hall toward his room)* I called and then changed my mind and said I didn't when I did, and since when is there anything wrong in that? It would mean only that I have a little problem of ambivalence. I got a minor problem of ambiguity goin' for me here, is all, and you're exaggerating everything all out of proportion. You're distorting everything! All of you! *(And he whirls to leave.)* If I have to lie to live, I will! *(He runs.)*

HARRIET. Where are you going? Come back here, Ozzie. Where are you going?

OZZIE. Kitchen. Kitchen.

He gallops away and out the front door. Blackout. Music.

Lights up. Bright afternoon. Harriet is alone, dusting. Rick, carrying books, enters from the kitchen and heads for the stairs to go to his room.

HARRIET. One day, Ricky . . . there were these two kittens and a puppy all in our back yard fighting. The kittens were little fur balls, so angry, and the little puppy, yapping and yapping. I was just a girl, but I picked them up in my arms. I held them all in my arms and they got very, very quiet.

RICK. I'm going up to my bedroom and study my history and English and trigonometry, Mom.

HARRIET. Do you know, I've called Father Donald seven times now—seven times, and haven't got an answer. Isn't that funny? He's starting to act like Jesus. You never hear from him. Isn't that funny? .

RICK. I'm going up to my bedroom and study my history and English and trigonometry, Mom, okay?

HARRIET. Fine, Ricky. Look in on David, would you?

RICK. Sure.

HARRIET. Good night.

RICK, *calling as he passes David's door.* Hi, Dave.

DAVID. Hi, Rick.

RICK. DAVE'S OKAY, MOM.

She is at the foot of the stairs. Rick goes from view. She turns back to her work, and the front door opens and Ozzie enters.

OZZIE, *excited, upset.* Harriet! Can you guess what happened? You'll never guess what happened.

(She continues cleaning.)

Harriet, wait. Stop.

HARRIET. Ozzie, I've got work to do.

OZZIE. But I want to tell you something.

HARRIET. All right, tell me; I can clean and listen; I can do both.

As she moves away, he rushes toward her, stretching out the lapel of his jacket to show her a large stain on it. She must see.

OZZIE. Lookit; look at that. What do you think that is? That spot on my coat, do you see it? That yellow?

HARRIET, *distressed, touching the spot.* Ohhhh, Ozzie! . . .

OZZIE. And the red mark on my neck.

HARRIET, *wincing.* Ohh, Ozzie, what happened? A bee sting! You got stung by a bee!

OZZIE. No, no; I was walking—thinking—trying to solve our problems. Somebody hit me with an egg. They threw it at me. I got hit with an egg.

(She stares, incredulous.)

That's right. I was just walking down the street and—bang—I was hit. I almost blacked out; I almost fell down.

HARRIET. Ozzie, my God, who would do such a thing?

OZZIE. I don't know. That's the whole point. I've racked my brain to understand and I can't. I was just walking along. That's all I was doing.

HARRIET. You mean you didn't even see them?

OZZIE, *pacing, his excitement growing.* They were in a car. I saw the car. And I saw the hand, too. A hand. Somebody's hand. A very large hand. Incredibly large.

HARRIET. What kind of car?

OZZIE. I don't know. An old one—black—big high fenders.

HARRIET. A Buick.

OZZIE. I think so; yes. Cruising up and down, up and down.

HARRIET. Was it near here? Why don't you sit down? *(Trying to help him sit, to calm and comfort him)* Sit down. Relax.

He obeys, hardly aware of what he is doing, sort of squatting on the couch, his body rigid with tension, as the story obsesses him.

OZZIE. And I heard them, too. They were hollering.

HARRIET. What did they say?

OZZIE. I don't know. It was just all noise. I couldn't understand.

HARRIET, *as if the realization doubles the horror.* It was more than one? My God!

OZZIE. I don't know. Two at least, at the very least. One to drive and one to throw. Maybe even three. A lookout sort of, peering up and down, and then he sees me. "There," he says; he points me out. I'm strolling along like a stupid ass, I don't even see them. The driver picks up speed.

(And now he is rising from the couch, reliving the story, cocking his arm.)

The thrower cocks his arm . . .

HARRIET. Ozzie, please, can't you relax? You look awful.

OZZIE. Nooo, I can't relax, goddamnit!

Off he goes, pacing again.

HARRIET. You look all flushed and sweating; please.

OZZIE. It just makes me so goddamn mad the more I think about it. It really does. GODDAMNIT! GODDAMNIT!

HARRIET. Oh, you poor thing.

OZZIE. Because it was calculated; it was calculated, Harriet, because that egg had been boiled to just the right point so it was hard enough to hurt but not so hard it wouldn't splatter. The filthy sonsabitches, but I'm gonna find 'em, I swear that to God, I'm gonna find 'em. I'm gonna kill 'em. I'm gonna cut out their hearts!

Rick appears at the top of the stairs.

RICK. Hey! What's all the racket? What's—

OZZIE. Ricky, come down here! . . . Goddamn 'em. . . .

HARRIET. Ricky, somebody hit your father with an egg!

RICK. Hit him? *(Descending hurriedly, worried)* Hit Dad?

OZZIE. They just threw it! Where's Dave? Dave here?

(He is suddenly looking around, moving for the stairs.)

I wanna tell Dave. DAVE!

HARRIET. Ozzie, give me your jacket!

She follows him part way up the stairs, tugging at the jacket.

OZZIE. I wanna tell Dave!

He and Harriet struggle to get the jacket off.

HARRIET. I'll take the spot off.

OZZIE. I gotta tell ole Dave!

(And the jacket is in her arms. He races on up the stairs.)

DAVE? DAVE! HEY, DAVE?

But David is not in his room. While Harriet descends and goes to a wall counter with drawers, Ozzie hurries off down the hallway. From a drawer Harriet takes a spray container and begins to clean the jacket.

RICK, *wandering near to her.* Boy, that's something, huh. What you got there, Mom?

HARRIET *(as Rick watches).* Meyer Spot Remover, do you know it? It gives just a sprinkling . . . like snow, which brushed away, leaves the fabric clean and fresh like spring.

Ozzie and David rush out from the hallway and down the stairs. Rick moves toward them to take a picture.

OZZIE. But it happened—and then there's this car tearin' off up the street. "Christ Jesus," I said, "I just been hit with an egg. Jesus Christ, that's impossible." And the way I felt—the way I feel— Harriet, let's have some beer; let's have some good beer for the boys and me.

(With a sigh, she moves to obey. As Ozzie continues, she brings beer, she brings peanuts. Ozzie now is pleased with his high energy, with his being the center of attention.)

It took me back to when I was a kid. Ole Fat Kramer. He lived on my street and we used to fight every day. For fun. Monday he'd win, and Tuesday, I'd beat him silly, my knees on his shoulders, blam, blam, blam. Later on, he grew up, became a merchant marine, sailed all over the world, and then he used to race sailboats up and down both coasts—he had one he lived on— anything that floated, he wanted to sail. And he wasn't fat either. We just called him that . . . and boy, oh boy, if he was around now—ohhhh, would we go get those punks threw that egg at me. We'd run 'em into the ground. We'd kill 'em like dogs . . . poor little stupid ugly dogs, we'd cut out their hearts.

RICK, *suddenly coughing and coughing—having gulped down beer —and getting to his feet.* Excuse me, Dad; excuse me. Listen, I've got to get going. You don't mind, do you? Got places to go; you're just talking nonsense anyway. (*He moves for the front door.*)

HARRIET. Have a good time, Rick.

RICK. I'm too pretty not to, Mom! (*And he is gone.*)

OZZIE. Where is . . . he . . . going? Where does he always go? Why does he always go and have some place to go? Always! . . .

HARRIET. Just you never mind, Ozzie. He's young and you're not. I'm going to do the dishes, but you just go right ahead with your little story and I'll listen from the kitchen.

Gathering the beer and glasses, she goes.

OZZIE, *following a little after her, not knowing quite what to do.* I . . . outran a bowling ball. . . . They bet I couldn't.

(*And he starts as if at a sound. He turns toward David.*)

What are you . . . looking . . . at? What do you think you're seeing?

DAVID. I'm not looking.

OZZIE. I feel watched; looked at.

DAVID. No.

OZZIE. Observed.

DAVID. I'm blind.

OZZIE. Did you do it? Had you anything to do with it?

DAVID. What?

OZZIE. That egg.

DAVID. I can't see.

OZZIE. I think you did. I feel like you did it.

DAVID. I don't have a car. I can't drive. How could I?

HARRIET, *hurrying in to clean up more of the party leftovers.* Ohh, it's so good to hear men's voices in the house again, my two favorite men in all the world—it's what I live for really. Would you like some coffee? Oh, of course you would. Let me put some on. Your humble servant at your command; I do your bidding, bid me be gone.

And she is gone without a pause, leaving Ozzie staring after her.

OZZIE. I could run again if I wanted. I'd . . . like . . . to want to. Christ, Fat Kramer is probably dead . . . now . . . not bouncing about in the ocean in some rattletrap, tin-can joke of a ship . . . but dust . . . locked in a box . . . held in old . . . cold hands. . . . And I just stand here, don't I? and let you talk any way you want. And Ricky gets up in the middle of some sentence I'm saying and walks right out and I let him. Because I fear him as I fear her . . . and you. Because I know the time is close when I will be of no use to any of you any longer . . . and I am so frightened that if I do not seem inoffensive . . . and pleasant . . . if I am not careful to never disturb any of you unnecessarily, you will all abandon me. I can no longer compel recognition. I can no longer impose myself, make myself seen.

HARRIET, *entering now happily with a tray of coffee.* Here you go. One for each and tea for me. Cream for David . . . *(Setting a cup for David, moving toward Ozzie)* and cream and sugar for—

OZZIE. Christ how you must have beguiled me!

HARRIET. Pardon?

OZZIE. Beguiled and deceived!

HARRIET. Pardon . . . Ozzie? . . .

OZZIE. And I don't even remember. I say "must" because I don't remember, I was so innocent, so childish in my strength, never seeing that it was surrendering I was doing, innocently and easily giving to you the love that was to return in time as flesh to imprison, detain, disarm and begin . . . to kill.

HARRIET, *examining him, scolding him.* Ozzie, how many beers have you had? You've had too many beers!

OZZIE. Get away!

(He whirls to point at David who sits on the floor facing upstage.)

Shut up! You've said enough! Detain and kill! Take and give nothing. It's what you meant, isn't it. You said it yesterday, a warning, nearly exactly this. This is your meaning!

DAVID. You're doing so well, Dad.

OZZIE, *not understanding.* What?

DAVID. You're doing so well.

OZZIE. No.

DAVID. You are.

OZZIE. Nooo, I'm doing awful. I'm doing terrible.

DAVID. This is the way you start, Dad. We'll be runners. Dad and Dave!

OZZIE. What's he saying?

HARRIET. My God, you're shaking; you're shaking.

OZZIE. I don't know what he's talking about. What's he talking about? *(To Harriet)* Just let me alone. Just please let me be. I don't really mean these things I'm saying. They're not really important. They'll go away and I don't mean them; they're just coming out of me; I'm just saying them, but I don't mean them. Oh, please, please, go away.

And David, behind them, pivots to go up the stairs. She whirls, drawn by his sudden movement.

HARRIET, *dismayed.* David? . . .

DAVID. I'm going upstairs.

HARRIET. Oh, yes. Of course, of course.

DAVID. Just for a while.

HARRIET. Fine. Good. Of course.

DAVID. I'll see you all later.

And he quietly enters his room, lies down.

OZZIE, *coiled on the couch, constricted with pain.* I remember . . . there was a day . . . when I wanted to leave you, all of you, and I wanted desperately to leave, and Hank was there . . . with me. We'd been playing cards. "No," he told me. "No," I couldn't, he said. "Think of the children," he said. He meant something by that. He meant something and I understood it. But now . . . I don't. I no longer have it—that understanding. It's left me. What did he mean?

HARRIET, *approaching, a little fearful.* You're trembling again. Look at you.

OZZIE. For a while . . . just a while, stay away. That's all I ask.

HARRIET, *reaching to touch him.* What?

OZZIE. Stay the hell away from me!

HARRIET. Stay away? How far away? Ozzie, how far away? I'll move over . . . (*And she scurries, frightened.*) . . . here. Is this far enough away? Ozzie . . .

OZZIE. It's my hands, my feet. There's tiredness in me. I wake up each morning, it's in my fingers . . . sleep. . . .

HARRIET. Ohhh, it's such a hateful thing in you the way you have no love for people different than yourself . . . even when your son has come home to tell you of them. You have no right to carry on this way. He didn't bring her back—didn't marry her— we have those two things to thank God for. You've got to stop thinking only of yourself. We don't matter, only the children. When are you going to straighten out your thinking? Promise. You've got to straighten out your thinking.

OZZIE. I do. I know.

HARRIET. We don't matter; we're nothing. You're nothing, Ozzie. Only the children.

OZZIE. I know. I promise.

HARRIET, *moving toward the stairs.* All right . . . just . . . rest . . . for a little; I'll be back. . . .

OZZIE. I promise, Harriet.

HARRIET, *more to herself than to him.* I'll go see how he is.

OZZIE, *coiled on the couch.* It's my hands; they hurt . . . I want to wrap them; my feet . . .

HARRIET. I'll tell him for you. I'll explain—how you didn't mean those terrible things you said. I'll explain.

OZZIE. It's going to be so cold; and I hurt . . . already. . . . So cold; my ankles! . . .

HARRIET, *hesitating on the stairway.* Oh, Ozzie, Ozzie, we're all so worried, but I just think we must hope for the fine bright day coming when we'll be a family again, as long as we try for what is good, truly for one another, please.

And she goes upstairs. The front door pops open.

RICK. Hi, Mom. Hi, Dad.

OZZIE. Hi, Rick. Your mom's upstairs. You have a nice time? I bet you did.

RICK. Fine; sure. How about you?

OZZIE. Fine; sure.

RICK. Whata you doin', restin'?

OZZIE. Workin'. Measurin'. Not everybody can play the guitar, *you know.* I'm going to build a wall . . . I think—a wall. Pretty soon . . . or . . . six walls. Thinkin' through the blueprints, lookin' over the plans.

RICK, *moving for the kitchen.* I'm gonna get some fudge, Dad; you want some?

OZZIE. No. Too busy.

RICK. I had the greatest piece a tail tonight, Dad; I really did. What a beautiful piece a ass.

OZZIE. Did you, Rick?

RICK. She was beee-uuuuu-ti-ful.

OZZIE. Who was it?

RICK. Nobody you'd know, Dad.

OZZIE. Oh. Where'd you do it—I mean, get it.

RICK. In her car.

OZZIE. You were careful, I hope.

RICK, *laughing a little.* C'mon, Dad.

OZZIE. I mean, it wasn't any decent girl.

RICK. Hell, no. . . .

He is still laughing, as Ozzie gets to his feet.

OZZIE, *starting for the door.* Had a dream of the guitar last night, Rick. It was huge as a building—all flecked with ice. You swung it in the air and I exploded.

RICK. I did?

OZZIE. Yes. I was gone.

RICK. Fantastic.

OZZIE, *exaggeratedly happy, almost singing.* Good night.

Ozzie is gone out the door. Blackout. Music.

Late night. Harriet comes down the hall toward David's room. She is wearing a bathrobe and carries a towel, soap, a basin of water. Giving just the lightest tap on the door, she enters, smiling.

HARRIET. A little bath . . . David? A little sponge bath, all right? You must be all hot and sticky always in that bed. And we can talk. Why don't you take your shirt off? We've an awful lot to talk about. Take your shirt off, David. Your poor father . . . he has no patience, no strength. Something has to be done. . . . A little sponge bath would be so nice. Have you talked to him lately? I think he thinks you're angry, for instance, with . . . us . . . for some reason . . . I don't know. (*Tugging at his shirt a little*) Take your shirt off, David. You'll feel cool. That's all we've ever wanted, your father and me—good sweet things for you and Rick—ease and lovely children, a car, a wife, a good job. Time to relax and go to church on Sundays . . . and on holidays all the children and grandchildren come together, mingling. It would be so wonderful—everyone so happy—turkey. Twinkling lights! (*She is puzzled, a little worried.*) David, are you going to take your shirt off for me?

DAVID. They hit their children, did you know that? They hit them with sticks.

HARRIET. What?

DAVID. The yellow people. They punish the disobedience of their children with sticks. And then they sleep together, one family in a bed, limbs all entwined like puppies. They work. I've seen them

. . . laugh. They go on picnics. They murder—out of petty jeal-
ousy. Young girls wet their cunts with spit when they are dry
from wear and yet another GI stands in line. They spit on their
hands and rub themselves, smiling, opening their arms.

HARRIET. That's not true.

DAVID. I saw—

HARRIET, *smilingly scolding him.* None of what you say. No. No.
All you did was something normal and regular, can't you see?
And hundreds of boys have done it before you. Thousands and
thousands. Even now. Now. Now. Why do you have to be so sick
and morbid about something so ordinary?

DAVID. She wasn't always a whore. Not always. Not—

HARRIET. If she is now, she was then, only you didn't know. You
didn't know.

*(She is reaching for him. He eludes her, stands above her, as she
is left sitting on the bed, looking up.)*

Oh, David, David, I'm sure she was a lovely little girl, but I
would be insane if I didn't want you to marry someone of your
own with whom you could be happy, if I didn't want grandchildren who could be free and welcome in their world. I couldn't
want anything else and still think I loved you. David, think of
their faces, their poor funny little faces. . . .

*And the cane is moving, slowly moving along the floor; it grazes
her ankle.*

DAVID. I know . . . I know. . . .

*The cane moves now along her inner calf, rising under the hem
of her robe, lifting. She tries to ignore it.*

HARRIET. The human face was not meant to be that way. A nose is
a thinness—you know that. And lips that are not thin are ugly,
and it is we who disappear, David. They don't change, and we
are gone. It is our triumph, our whiteness. We disappear. What
are you doing?

*(The cane has driven her back along the bed; no longer can it be
ignored. It has pressed against her.)*

They take us back and down if our children are theirs—it is not a mingling of blood, it is theft.

(*And she hits the cane away. In revulsion she stands, wanting only to flee.*)

Oh, you don't mean these awful things you do. Your room stinks—odors come from under the door. You don't clean yourself. David, David, you've lost someone you love and it's pain for you, don't you see? I know, I know. But we will be the same, lost from you—you from us—and what will that gain for anyone? What?

Now the cane begins to scrape along the floor. It begins to lift toward her, and, shuddering, she flees down the hall. David opens the door, listens. Stepping into the hall, he carefully shuts the door before moving down the stairs. In the living room, he moves to plant himself before the front door. Harriet, wearing a raincoat over her robe and a scarf on her head, comes down the stairs, when she turns toward the door and she sees David, she stops, nods hello, and stands as he begins to advance upon her.

DAVID. Do you remember? It was a Sunday when we had all gone to church and there was a young man there with his yellow wife and child. You spoke to us . . . Dad and Rick and me, as if we were conspirators. "I feel so sorry for that poor man—the baby looks like *her*," you said, and your mouth twisted as if you had been forced to swallow someone else's spit.

HARRIET. No, no. You want only to hurt us, don't you? Isn't that right? That's all you want. Only to give us unhappiness. You cheat her, David. That lovely, lovely little girl you spoke of. She merits more to be done in her memory than cruelty.

She has seated herself on the couch, clinging to some kind of normalcy, an odd and eerie calmness on both of them now.

DAVID. And I felt that I must go to her if I was to ever live, and I felt that to touch truly her secret stranger's tongue and mind would kill me. Now she will not forgive the way I was.

HARRIET, *standing up.* No. No, no. No, you don't know how badly I feel. I've got a fever, the start of a cold or flu. Let me be. I can't hardly . . . (*And she is moving away from him, back toward the stairs*) move . . . or stand up. I just want to flop somewhere and not have to move. I'm so weak . . . don't hurt me anymore. Don't hurt me—no more—I've got fever; please, fever; don't hurt me. (*She is on the stairs.*)

DAVID. But I have so much to show you.

HARRIET—*stops to stare helplessly down at him.* Who are you? I don't know who you are.

DAVID. David.

HARRIET. Noooooo.

DAVID. But I am.

HARRIET. No, no. Oh, no.

Moving now as in a trance, she walks up the stairs and down the hallway, all slowly, while Zung comes forward in David's room, and David, in the living room, calls after his mother.

DAVID. But it's what you want, don't you see? You can see it. Her wrists are bound in coils of flowers. Flowers are strung in her hair. She hangs from the wind and men strike and kick her. They are blind so that they may not see her, yet they howl, wanting not to hurt her but only as I do, to touch and hold her . . . and they howl. I'm home. Little David. . . . Home.

(*And he is turning now to take possession of the house. As he speaks, he moves to take the space. A conquerer, he parades in the streets he has taken; among the chairs, around the lamp.*)

Little Davey . . . of all the toys and tops and sailor suits, the plastic cars and Tinkertoys. Drum-player, bed-wetter, home-run-hitter, I'm home . . . now . . . and I want to drink from the toilet, wash there.

(*As he climbs the stairs, he passes by Zung, who stands in his room looking out at him. He walks on down the hall in the direction Harriet fled.*)

And you will join me. You . . . will . . . join me!

When he has gone, Zung sits to gaze down upon the living

room, *as the front door opens. Ozzie, dressed in a suit or perhaps even a tuxedo, enters from the outside. Under his arm he carries a packet of several hundred sheets of paper. He moves now with an absolute confidence, almost smugness, as he carefully sets down the papers and proceeds to arrange three items of furniture—perhaps two chairs and a footstool—in such a way that they face him. He is cocky. Now he addresses them.*

OZZIE, *to the large chair.* Harriet. . . . *(Nodding to the second chair)* David. . . . *(Patting the footstool)* Ricky.

(He looks them over, the three empty chairs, and then speaks in the manner of a chairman of the board addressing the members of his board, explaining his position and plan of action for total solution. This is a kind of commercial on the value of Ozzie.)

I'm glad we've gotten finally together here, because the thing I've decided to do—and you all, hopefully, will understand my reasoning—is to *combat* the weariness beginning in me. It's like stepping into a hole, the way I feel each morning when I awaken, I see the day and the sun and I'm looking upward into the sky with a sense of looking down. A sense of hovering over a great pit into which I am about to fall. The sky. Foolishness and deceit, you say, and I know you're right—a trick of feeling inside me being played against me, seeking to diminish me and increase itself until it is larger than me filling me and who will I be then? It. That feeling of being nothing. At first . . . at first . . . I thought the thing to do would be to learn the guitar. . . . But *that* I realized in just the nick of time was a folly that would have taken me into the very agony of frustration I was seeking to avoid. The skill to play like Ricky does is a great gift and only Ricky has it. He has no acids rotting his heart. He is all lies and music, his brain small and scaly, the brain of a snake forever innocent of the fact that it crawls. Lucky Ricky. But there are other things that people can do. And I've come at last to see the one that I must try if I am to become strong again in my opinion of myself. *(Holding up, with great confidence, one of the many packets of paper)* What I have here is an inventory of everything I own. Everything. Every stick of furniture, pot and pan, every sock, T-shirt, pen or pencil. And opposite is its price. For instance—here

—that davenport—five hundred an' twelve dollars an' ninety-eight cents. That chair—a hundred twenty ninety-nine. That table . . . (*He hurries to the table.*) . . . this table—thirty-two twenty-nine. Et cetera. Et cetera. Now the idea is that you each carry a number of these at all times.

(*He is distributing more papers to the chairs, his control, however, diminishing, so that the papers are thrown about.*)

Two or three copies at all times, and you are to pass them out at the slightest provocation. Let people know who I am, what I've done. Someone says to you, "Who are you?" You say, "I'm Ozzie's son." "I'm Ozzie's wife." Who?" they'll say. "Take a look at that!" you tell 'em. Spit it out, give 'em a copy, turn on your heel and walk right out. That's the way I want it; from all of you from here on out, that's the WAY I WANT IT!

(*And the room goes suddenly into eerie light. Zung, high behind him in David's room, is hit with a sudden light that makes Ozzie go rigid, as if some current from her has entered into him, and he turns slowly to look up at her.*)

Let him alone. Let David alone.

Harriet is in the hallway.

HARRIET. Is there any aspirin down there? I don't feel well . . . Ozzie. I don't feel well at all. David poked me with his cane and I don't like . . . what's . . . going on.

(*Ozzie is only staring at Zung.*)

I don't want what's happening to happen.

(*She has halted on the stairway.*)

It must be some awful flu, I'm so weak, or some awful cold. There's an odor . . .

OZZIE. I'll go to the drugstore. My eyes hurt; funny . . .

HARRIET. Oh, Ozzie . . . oh my God. It was awful. I can't help it. He's crazy—he—

OZZIE. I don't want to hear about him. I don't want to hear. Oh, no, oh, no. I can't. No more, no more. Let him do what he wants. No more of him, no more. Just you—you're all that I can see. All that I care for or want.

He has moved to her as she moved down, and they embrace.

HARRIET. David's crazy! . . .

OZZIE. You're everything.

HARRIET. Please . . .

OZZIE. Listen; we must hide; please.

HARRIET, *moving to kneel and he, while helping her, kneels also.* Pray with me.

OZZIE. We won't move. We'll hide by not moving.

HARRIET. We must beg God to not turn against him; convince him. Ozzie, pray. . . .

OZZIE. Yes! . . .

HARRIET. Now! . . .

They pray: kneeling, murmuring, and it goes on and on. The front door opens.

RICK. Hi, Mom. Hi, Dad.

(They continue. He stops.)

Hi . . . Mom. Hi, Dad. . . . *(very puzzled)* Hi . . . Mom. . . . Hi . . . Dad. . . .

(He thinks and thinks.)

DAVID!

(He screams at David. He goes running up to look in David's room, but the room is empty. David, in ragged combat fatigues, appears on the top of the stairs. Rick, frightened, backs away.)

Dave . . . what have you got to say for yourself? What can you? Honest ta God, I've had it. I really have. I can't help it, even if you are sick, and I hate to complain, but you're getting them so mixed up they're not themselves anymore. Just a minute ago— one minute—they were on their knees, do you know that? Just a minute ago—right here on the living-room floor. Now what's the point of that? They're my mom and dad, too.

DAVID. He doesn't know, does he, Dad? Did you hear him?

RICK (*as Ozzie and Harriet are getting from their knees and struggling to sit on the couch*). Let Dad alone.

DAVID, *on the landing, looking down on them.* He doesn't know how when you finally see yourself, there's nothing really there to see . . . isn't that right? Mom?

RICK. Dave, honest to God, I'm warning you, let them alone.

David descends with Zung behind him. Calmly he speaks, growing slowly happy.

DAVID. Do you know how north of here, on farms, gentle loving dogs are raised, while in the forests, other dogs run wild? And upon occasion, one of those that's wild is captured and put in among the others that are tame, bringing with it the memory of when they had all been wild—the dark and terror—that had made them wolves. Don't you hear them?

And there is a rumbling.

RICK. What? Hear what?

It is windlike, the rumbling of many trucks.

DAVID. Don't you hear the trucks? They're all over town, lined up from the center of town into the country. Don't you hear? They've stopped bringing back the blind. They're bringing back the dead now. The convoy's broken up. There's no control . . . they're walking from house to house, through the shrubbery, under the trees, carrying one of the dead in a bright blue rubber bag for which they have no papers, no name or number. No one knows whose it is. They're at the Jensens' now. Now Al Jensen's at the door, all his kids behind him trying to peek. Al looks for a long, long time into the open bag before he shakes his head. They zipper shut the bag and turn away. They've been to the Mayers', the Kellys', the Irwins' and Kresses'. They'll be here soon.

OZZIE. Nooo.

DAVID. And Dad's going to let them in. We're going to let them in.

HARRIET. What's he saying?

DAVID. He's going to knock.

OZZIE. I DON'T KNOW.

DAVID. Yes. Yes.

A knocking sound. Is it David knocking with his fist against the door or table?

OZZIE. Nooooo.

RICK. Mom, he's driving Dad crazy.

Knocking loud: it seems to be at the front door.

OZZIE. David, will I die?

He moves toward the door.

HARRIET. Who do you suppose it could be so late?

RICK, *intercepting Ozzie, blocking the way to the door.* I don't think you should just go opening the door to anybody this time of the night, there's no telling who it might be.

DAVID. We know who it is.

OZZIE. Oh, David, why can't you wait? Why can't you rest?

But David is the father now, and he will explain. He loves them all.

DAVID. Look at her. See her, Dad. Tell her to go to the door. Tell her yes, it's your house, you want her to open the door and let them in. Tell her yes, the one with no name is ours. We'll put it in that chair. We can bring them all here. I want them all here, all the trucks and bodies. There's room. *(Handing Rick the guitar)* Ricky can sing. We'll stack them along the walls . . .

OZZIE. Nooo . . .

DAVID. Pile them over the floor . . .

OZZIE. No, no . . .

DAVID. They will become the floor and they will become the walls, the chairs. We'll sit in them; sleep. We will call them "home." We will give them as gifts—call them "ring" and "pot" and "cup." No, no; it's not a thing to fear. . . . We will notice them no more than all the others.

He is gentle, happy, consoling to them.

OZZIE. What others? There are no others. Oh . . . please die. Oh, wait. . . .

(And he scurries to the TV where it sits beneath the stairs.)

I'll get it fixed. I'll fix it. Who needs to hear it? We'll watch it. *(Wildly turning TV channels.)* I flick my rotten life. Oh, there's a good one. Look at that one. Ohhh, isn't that a good one? That's the best one. That's the best one.

DAVID. They will call it madness. We will call it seeing.

Calmly he lifts Ozzie.

OZZIE. I don't want to disappear.

DAVID. Let her take you to the door. We will be runners. You will have eyes.

OZZIE. I will be blind. I will disappear.

Knocking is heard again. Again.

DAVID. You stand and she stands. "Let her go," you say; "she is garbage and filth and you must get her back if you wish to live. She is sickness, I must cherish her." Old voices you have trusted all your life as if they were your own, speaking always friendly. "She's all of everything impossible made possible!"

OZZIE. Ricky . . . nooo! . . .

DAVID. Don't call to Ricky. You love her. You will embrace her, see her and—

OZZIE. He has no right to do this to me.

DAVID. Don't call to Ricky!

OZZIE, *suddenly raging, rushing at David, pushing him.* You have no right to do this.

RICK. Noooooo!

(Savagely he smashes his guitar down upon David, who crumples.)

Let Dad alone. Let him alone. He's sick of you. What the hell's the matter with you? He doesn't wanna talk anymore about all the stupid stuff you talk. He wants to talk about cake and cookies and cars and coffee. He's sick a you and he wants you to shut up. We hate you, goddamn you.

Silence: David lies still.

ZUNG. Chào ông!

(Ozzie pivots, looks at her.)

Chào ông! Hôm nay ông manh không?

OZZIE. Oh, what is it that you want? I'm tired. I mean it. Forgive me. I'm sick of the sight of you, squatting all the time. In filth like animals, talking gibberish, your breath sick with rot. . . . And yet you look at me with those sad pleading·eyes as if there is some real thing that can come between us when you're not even here. You are deceit.

(His hands, rising, have driven to her throat. The fingers close.)

I'm not David. I'm not silly and soft . . . little David. The sight of you sickens me. YOU HEAR ME, DAVID? Believe me. I am speaking my honest true feelings. I spit on you, the both of you; I piss on you and your eyes and pain. Flesh is lies. You are garbage and filth. You are darkness. I cast you down. Deceit. Animal. Dirty animal.

And he is over her. They are sprawled on the ground. Silence as no one moves. She lies like a rag beneath him.

RICK. I saw this really funny movie last night. This really . . . funny, funny movie about this young couple and they were going to get a divorce but they didn't. It was really funny.

Ozzie is hiding the girl. In a proscenium production, he can drag her behind the couch; in three-quarter, he covers her with a blanket brought to him by Harriet which matches the rug.

HARRIET. What's that? What's that?

RICK. This movie I saw.

HARRIET. Anybody want to go for groceries? We need Kleenex, sugar, milk.

RICK. What a really funny movie.

OZZIE. I'll go; I'll go.

HARRIET. Good. Good.

OZZIE. I think I saw it on TV.

They are cleaning up the house now, putting the chairs back in order, dumping all of Ozzie's leaflets in the waste can.

HARRIET. Did you enjoy it, Rick?

RICK. Oh, yeh. I loved it.

OZZIE. I laughed so much I almost got sick. It was really good. I laughed.

RICK. I bet it was; I bet you did.

OZZIE. Oh, I did.

Even David helps with the cleaning: he gets himself off the floor and seated in a chair.

HARRIET. How are you feeling, Ricky?

RICK. Fine.

HARRIET. Good.

RICK. How do you feel?

HARRIET. Oh, I'm all right. I feel fine.

OZZIE. Me, too. I feel fine, too. What day is it anyway? Monday?

HARRIET. Wednesday.

RICK. Tuesday, Mom.

Now all three are seated on the couch.

OZZIE. I thought it was Monday.

RICK. Oh, no.

HARRIET. No, no. You're home now, David. . . .

RICK, *moving to David, who sits alone in a chair.* Hey, Dave, listen, will you. I mean I know it's not my place to speak out and give advice and everything because I'm the youngest, but I just gotta say my honest true feelings and I'd kill myself if I were you, Dave. You're in too much misery. I'd cut my wrists. Honestly speaking, brother to brother, you should have done it long ago.

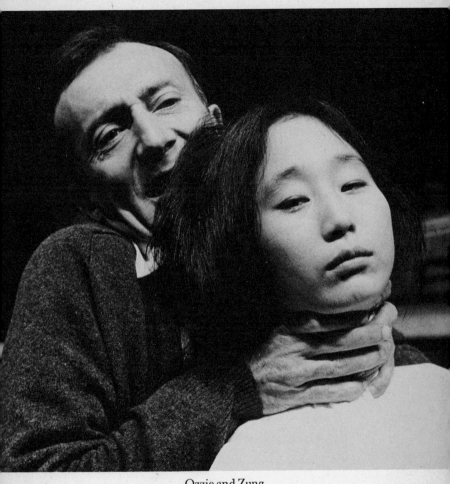

Ozzie and Zung

(David is looking about.)

You looking for her, Dave? You looking for her? She's not here.

DAVID. What?

RICK. Nooo. She's never been here. You just thought so. You decided not to bring her, Dave, remember? You decided, all things considered that you preferred to come back without her. Too much risk and inconvenience . . . you decided. Isn't that right? Sure. You know it is. You've always known.

(Silence. Harriet moves to look out the front door.)

Do you want to use my razor, Dave? *(Pulling a straight razor from his pocket)* I have one right here and you can use it if you want.

(David seems to be looking at the razor.)

Just take it if you want it, Dave.

HARRIET. Go ahead, David. The front yard's empty. You don't have to be afraid. The streets, too . . . still and empty.

RICK. It doesn't hurt like you think it will. Go ahead; just take it, Dave.

OZZIE. You might as well.

RICK. That's right.

OZZIE. You'll feel better.

RICK. I'll help you now, Dave, okay?

HARRIET. I'll go get some pans and towels.

RICK, *moving about David, patting him, buddying him.* Oh, you're so confused, you don't know what to do. It's just a good thing I got this razor, Boy, that's all I gotta say. You're so confused. You see, Dave, where you're wrong is your point of view, it's silly. It's just really comical because you think people are valuable or something and, given a chance like you were to mess with 'em, to take a young girl like that and turn her into a whore, you shouldn't, when of course you should or at least might . . . on whim . . . you see? I mean, you're all backwards, Dave—you're upside down. You don't know how to go easy and play—I bet you didn't have any fun the whole time you were over there—no fun at all—and it was there. I got this buddy Gerry, he was there, and he used to throw bags of cement at 'em from off the back a his truck. They'd go whizzin' through those villages, throwin' off these bags a cement. You could kill people, he says, you hit 'em right. Especially the kids. There was this once they knocked this ole man off his bicycle—fifty pounds a dry cement—and then the back a the truck got his legs. It was hysterical—can't you just see that, Dave? Him layin' there howlin', all the guys in the truck bowin' and wavin' and tippin' their hats. What a goddamn funny story, huh?

Harriet has brought silver pans and towels with roosters on them. The towels cover the arms of the chair and David's lap. The pans will catch the blood. All has been neatly placed. David, with Ricky's help, cuts one wrist, then the other, as they talk.

DAVID. I wanted . . . to kill you . . . all of you.

RICK. I know, I know; but you're hurt; too weak.

DAVID. I wanted for you to need what I had and I wouldn't give it.

HARRIET. That's not possible.

OZZIE. Nooooo.

DAVID. I wanted to get you. Like poor bug-eyed fish flung up from the brief water to the lasting dirt, I would gut you.

HARRIET. David, no, no, you didn't want that.

OZZIE. No, no.

RICK. I don't even know why you'd think you did.

OZZIE. We kill you is what happens.

RICK. That's right.

OZZIE. And then, of course, we die, too. . . . Later on, I mean. And nothing stops it. Not words . . . or walls . . . or even guitars.

RICK. Sure.

OZZIE. That's what happens.

HARRIET. It isn't too bad, is it?

RICK. How bad is it?

OZZIE. He's getting weaker.

HARRIET. And in a little, it'll all be over. You'll feel so grand. No more funny talk.

RICK. You can shower; put on clean clothes. I've got deodorant you can borrow. After Roses, Dave. The scent of a thousand roses.

He is preparing to take a picture—crouching, aiming.

HARRIET. Take off your glasses, David.

OZZIE. Do as you're told.

RICK (*as David's hands are rising toward the glasses to remove them*). I bet when you were away there was only plain water to wash in, huh? You prob'ly hadda wash in the rain.

(*He takes the picture; there is a flash. A slide appears on the screen: a close-up of David, nothing visible but his face. It is the slide that, appearing at the start of the play, was referred to as "somebody sick." Now it hovers, stricken, sightless, revealed.*)

Mom, I like David like this.

HARRIET. He's happier.

OZZIE. We're all happier.

RICK. Too bad he's gonna die.

OZZIE. No, no, he's not gonna die, Rick. He's only gonna nearly die. Only nearly.

RICK. Ohhhhhhhhhhh.

HARRIET. Mmmmmmmmmmmmmm.

And Rick, sitting, begins to play his guitar for David. The music is alive and fast. It has a rhythm, a drive of happiness that is contagious. The lights slowly fade.

AUTHOR'S NOTE

In any society there is an image of how the perfectly happy family should appear. It is this image that the people in this play wish to preserve above all else. Mom and Dad are not concerned that terrible events have occurred in the world, but rather that David has come home to behave in a manner that makes him no longer lovable. Thus he is keeping them from being the happy family they know they must be. He attacks those aspects of their self-image in which reside all their sense of value and sanity. But, curiously, one of the requisites of their self-image is that everything is fine, and, consequently, for a long time they must not even admit that David is attacking.

Yet everything is being communicated. Often a full, long speech is used in this play where in another, more "realistic" play there would be only a silence during which something was communicated between two people. Here the communication is obvious, because it is directly spoken. Consequently the ignoring of that which is communicated must be equally obvious. David throws a yelling, screaming tantrum over his feelings of isolation and Harriet confidently, cheerfully offers Ezy Sleep sleeping pills in full faith that they will solve his problem. The actors must try to look at what they are ignoring. They must not physically ignore things—turn their backs, avert their eyes, be busy with something else. The point is not that they do not physically see or hear, but that they psychologically ignore. Though they look right at things, though they listen closely, they do not see or hear. The harder they physically focus and concentrate on an event, the clearer their psychological state and the point and nature of the play will be, when in their next moments and speeches they verbally and emotionally ignore or miss what they have clearly looked at. In addition, the actors should try not to take the play overly seriously. The characters (except for David) do not take things seriously until they are forced to, and then they do it for as short a time as they can manage. Let the

audience take seriously the jolly way the people go about the curi-
ous business of their lives.

Stylization, then, is the main production problem. The forms referred to during the time of writing *Sticks and Bones* were farce,
horror movie, TV situation comedy. These should have their
effect, though it must be remembered that they are where form was
sought, not content. What is poetic in the writing must not be rein-
forced by deep feeling on the part of the actors, or the writing will
hollow into pretension. In a more "realistic" play, where language
is thinner, subtext must be supplied or there is no weight. Such
deep support of *Sticks and Bones* will make the play ponderous. As
a general rule, I think it is true that when an actor's first impulse
(the impulse of all his training) is to make a heavy or serious adjustment in a scene, he should reverse himself and head for a light-
hearted adjustment. If his first impulse is toward lightheartedness,
perhaps he should turn toward a serious tack. A major premise of
the play is that stubbing your own big toe is a more disturbing
event than hearing of a stranger's suicide.

At the start, the family is happy and orderly, and then David
comes home and he is unhappy. As the play progresses, he becomes
happier and they become unhappier. Then, at the end, they are
happy.

Sticks and Bones was first produced at Villanova University in 1969, under the direction of James J. Christy, with the following cast (listed in order of appearance):

OZZIE	Brian Morgan
HARRIET	Regina Res
RICK	Bill Hickey
SERGEANT MAJOR	Bob Delegall
DAVID	Edward Powers
GIRL	Kaity Tong
POLICEMAN	Paul Seymour
PRIEST	Mark McGovern

Sticks and Bones was first produced professionally by Joseph Papp, on November 7, 1971, at the New York Shakespeare Festival Public Theater, under the direction of Jeff Bleckner, with the following cast:

OZZIE	Tom Aldredge
HARRIET	Elizabeth Wilson
RICK	Cliff DeYoung
SERGEANT MAJOR	Hector Elias
DAVID	David Selby
GIRL	Asa Gim
PRIEST	Charles Siebert

Associate Producer, Bernard Gersten; set by Santo Loquasto; costumes by Theoni V. Aldredge; lighting by Ian Calderon.

Sticks and Bones was first produced on Broadway by Joseph Papp, on March 1, 1972, at the John Golden Theatre, under the direction of Jeff Bleckner, with the following cast:

OZZIE	Tom Aldredge
HARRIET	Elizabeth Wilson
PRIEST	Charles Siebert
RICK	Cliff DeYoung
SERGEANT MAJOR	Hector Elias
DAVID	Drew Snyder
GIRL	Asa Gim

Associate Producer, Bernard Gersten; set by Santo Loquasto; costumes by Theoni V. Aldredge; lighting by Ian Calderon.

A selection of books published by Penguin is listed on the following page.

For a complete list of books available from Penguin in the United States, write to Dept. DG, Penguin Books, 299 Murray Hill Parkway, East Rutherford, New Jersey 07073.

For a complete list of books available from Penguin in Canada, write to Penguin Books Canada Limited, 2801 John Street, Markham, Ontario L3R 1B4.